AF305324

THE ORDINARY AND THE ODD

Illustrations by Swen Swensøn

COLLECTIVE SHORTS
by NHP PUBLISHING

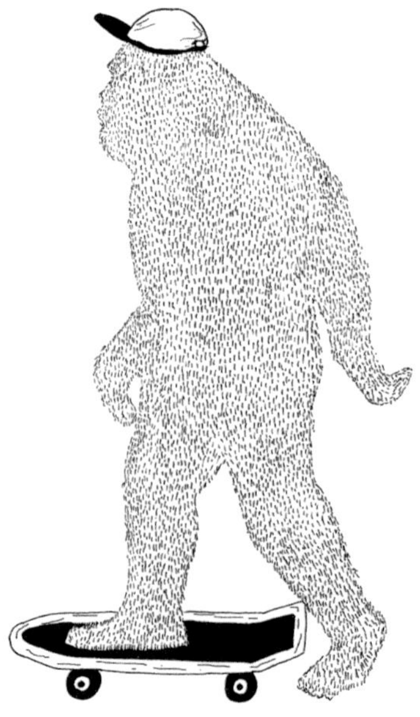

In this book I would like to show you how I perceive things. The details that surround us every day, that we pass without even noticing.

This book ought to slow things down.

I like to create positive feelings, as there already are too many bad things happening around us. I would like to invite people to sit back, relax and to enjoy the beautiful things in life.

Life is everywhere, beauty is everywhere. We only forgot to notice. This book captures the moment and invites the spectator to take a closer look, to take time and watch closely.

My artworks are centered on the beauty that lies in daily situations, although some of them may seem odd or not interesting at all. I always try to draw the spectator's attention towards what I see in it.

Some of my works tell stories, others tend to freeze the moment. I try to include everyone in my artworks and to leave enough space for individual interpretation.

The spectator is invited to spin on the story behind a picture, to reinterprete it or simply to be inspired by it. Although, some creations aren't as obvious or easy to grasp as they seem at first glance. Some details become visible only after a while.

In addition to the well known works, this book also includes a selection of not yet published and new works of mine. Including the central elements of beauty and wit, but also with a certain amount of drama overshadowing the bright and minimalist Scandinavian surroundings.

Enjoy!

Nature

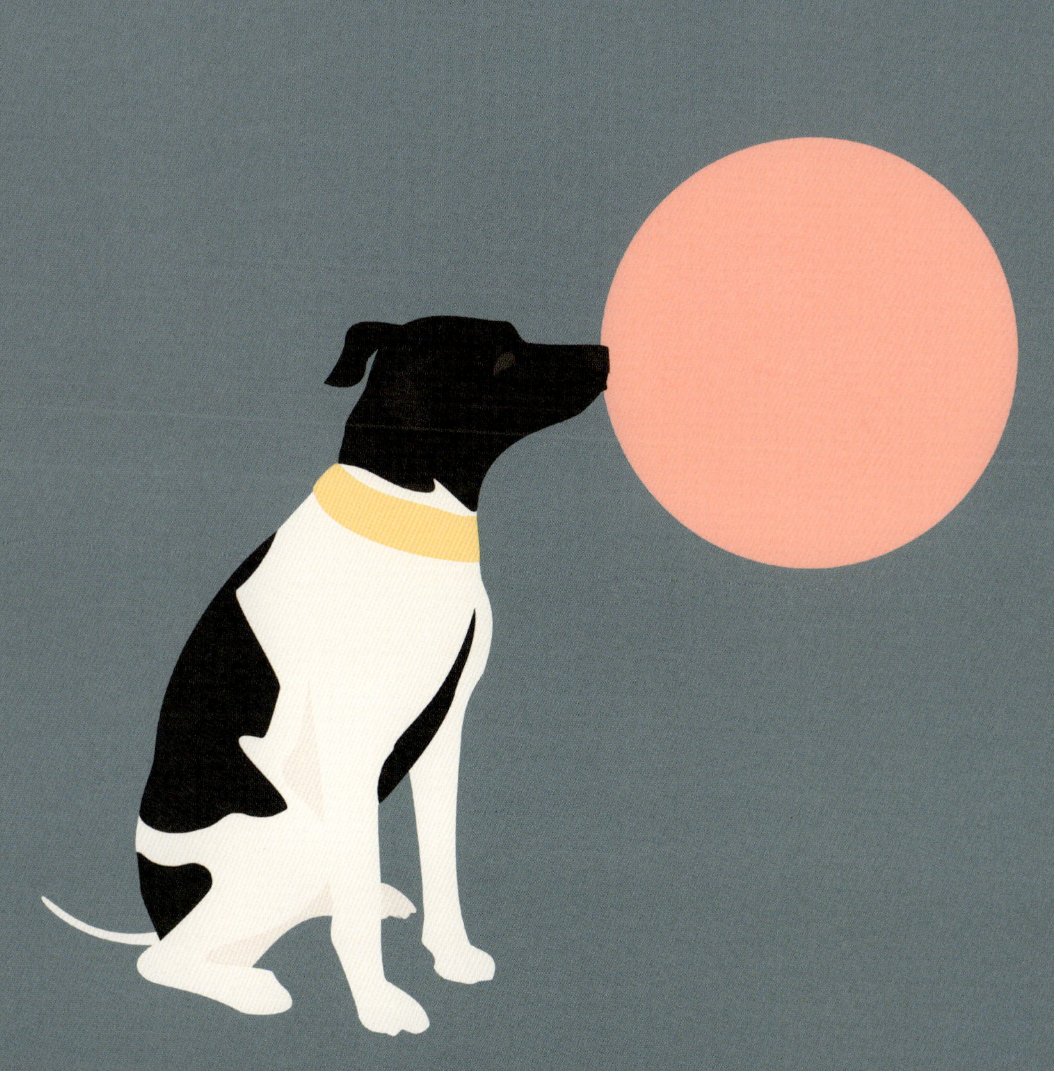

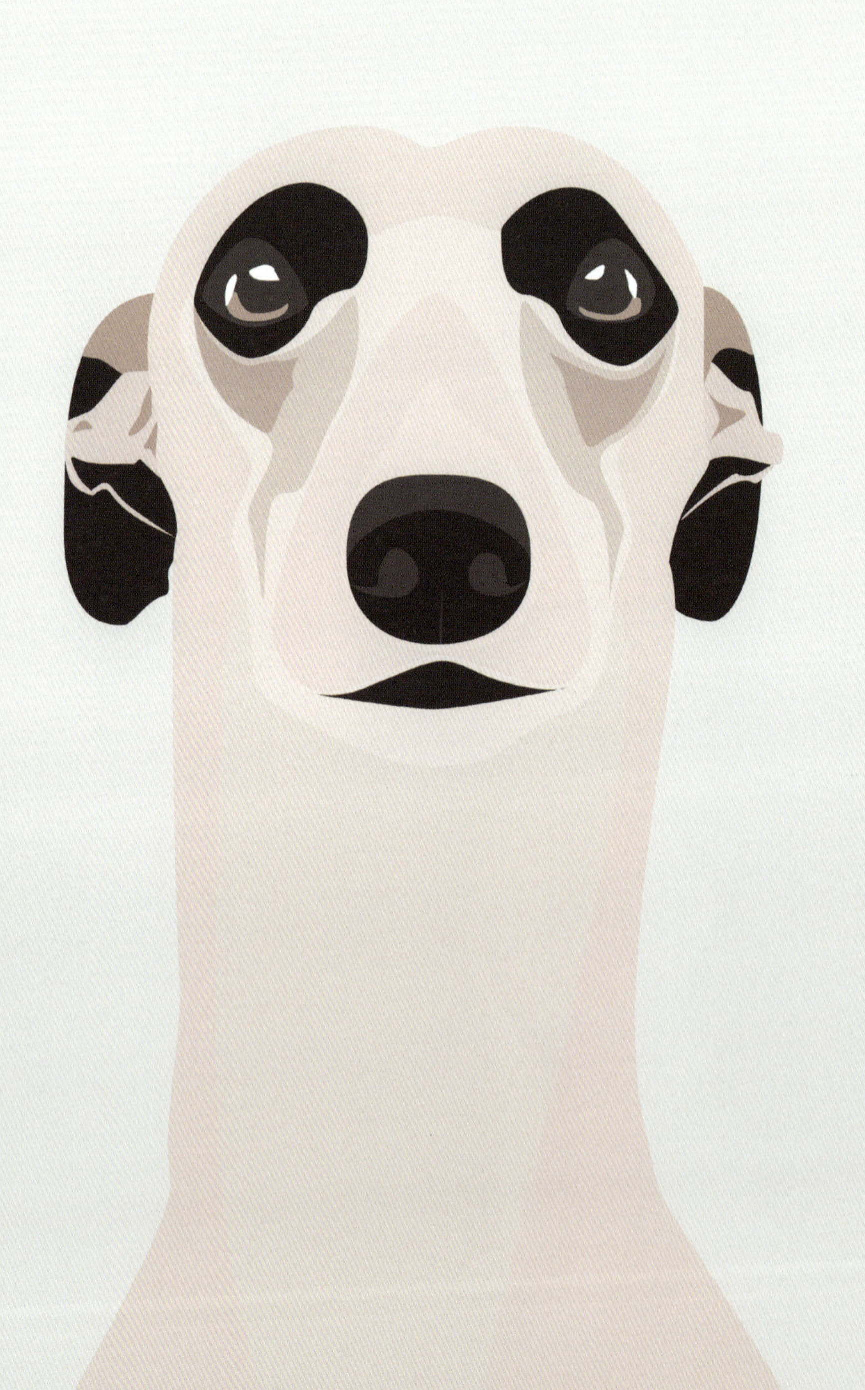

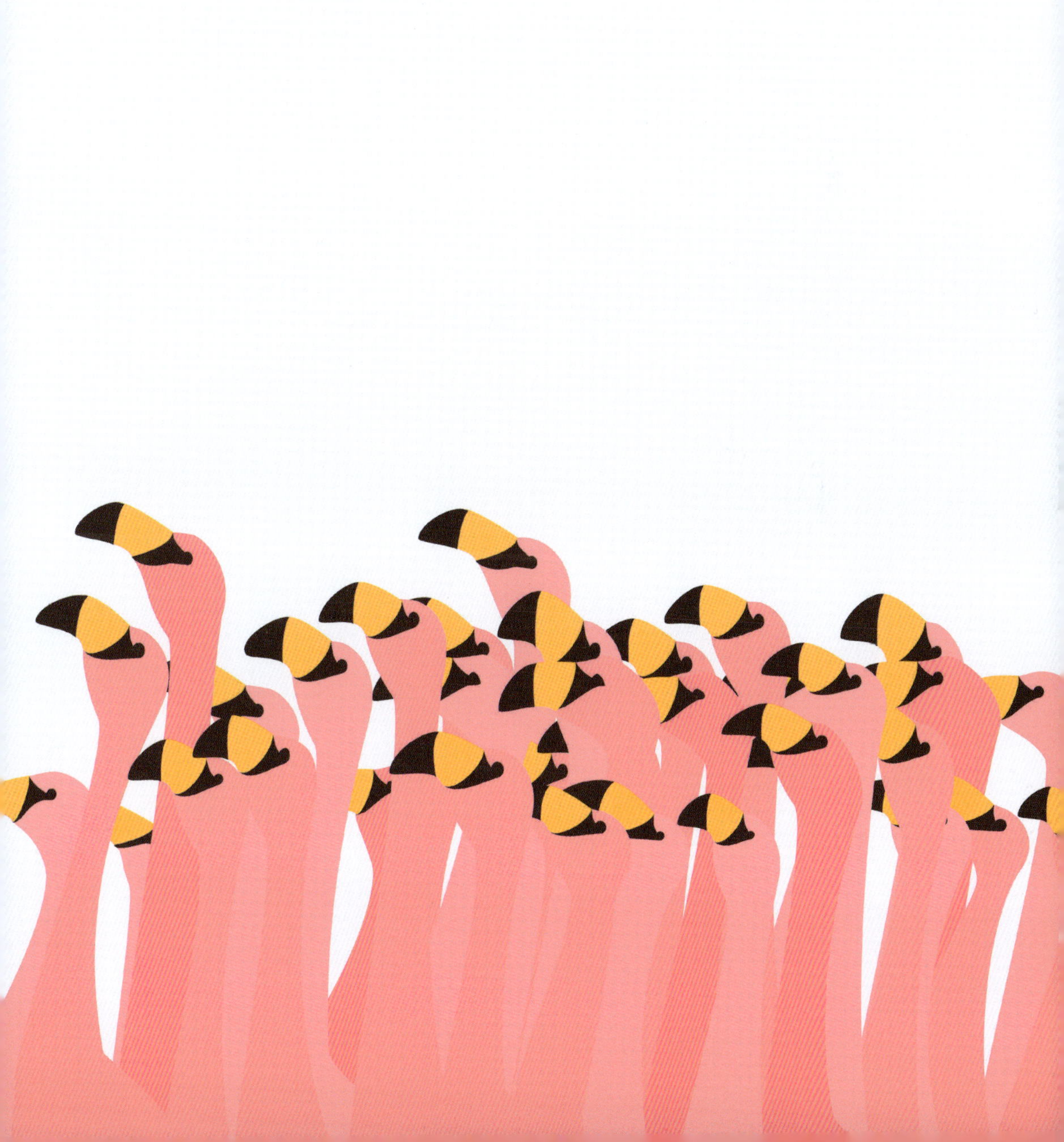

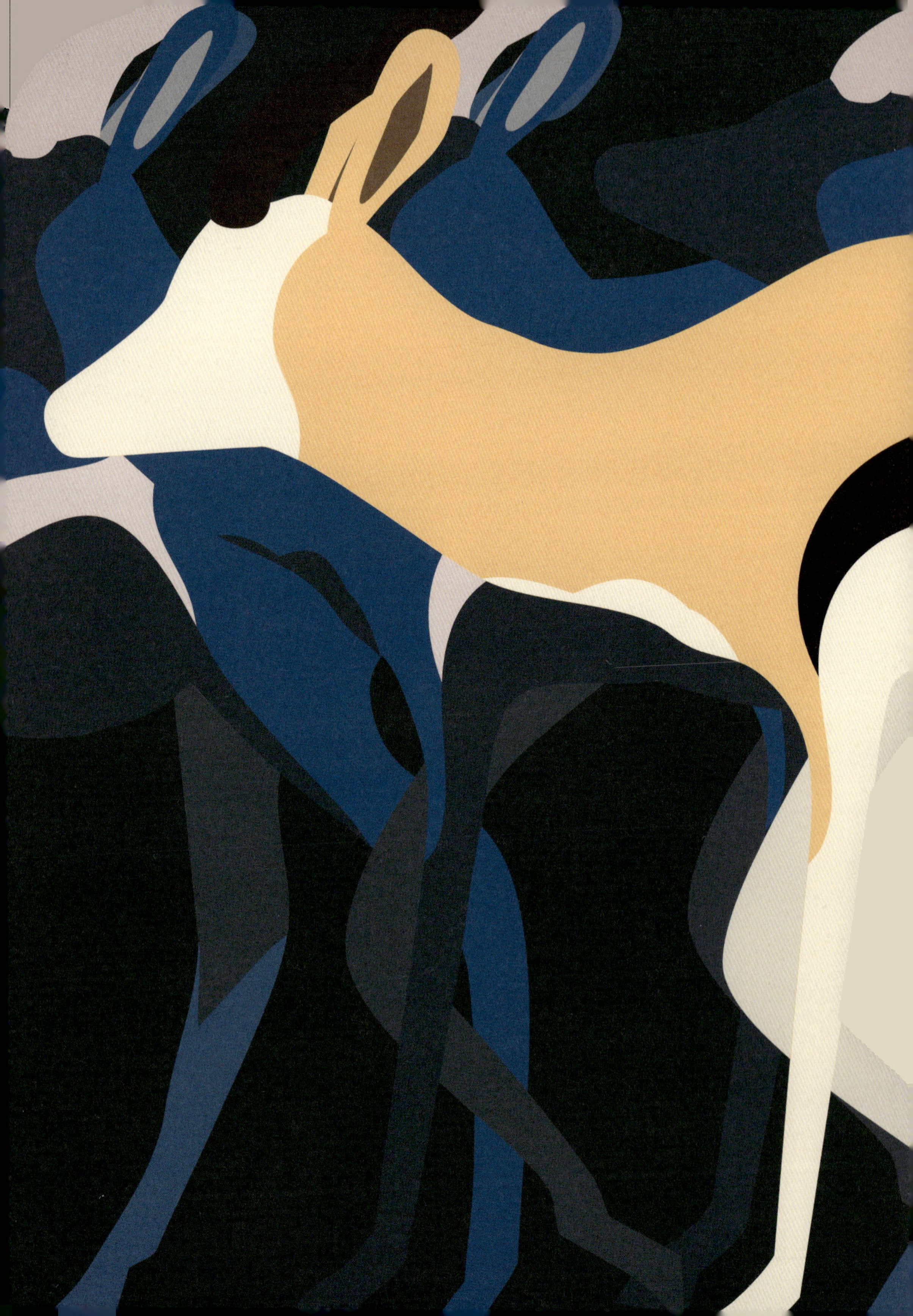

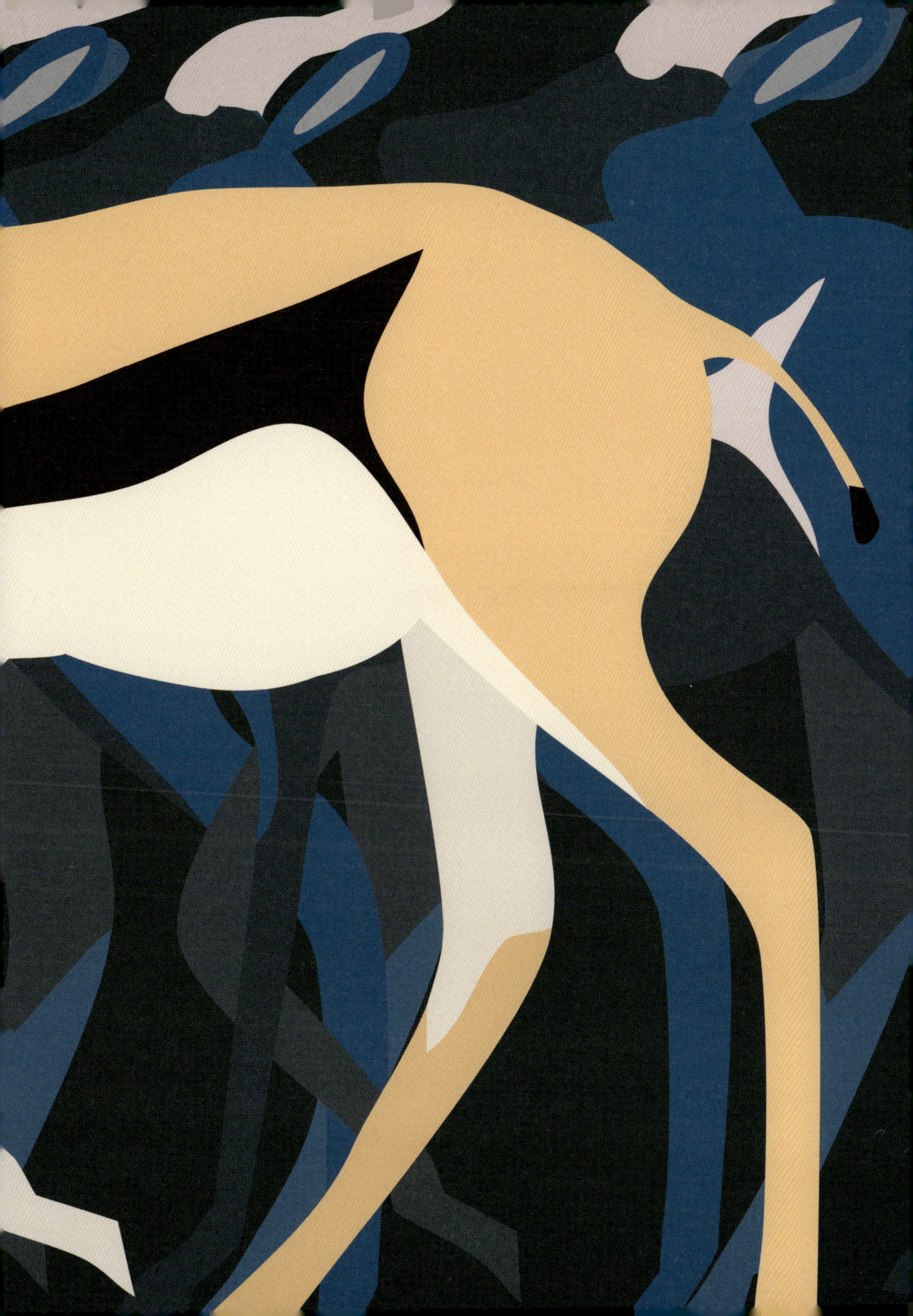

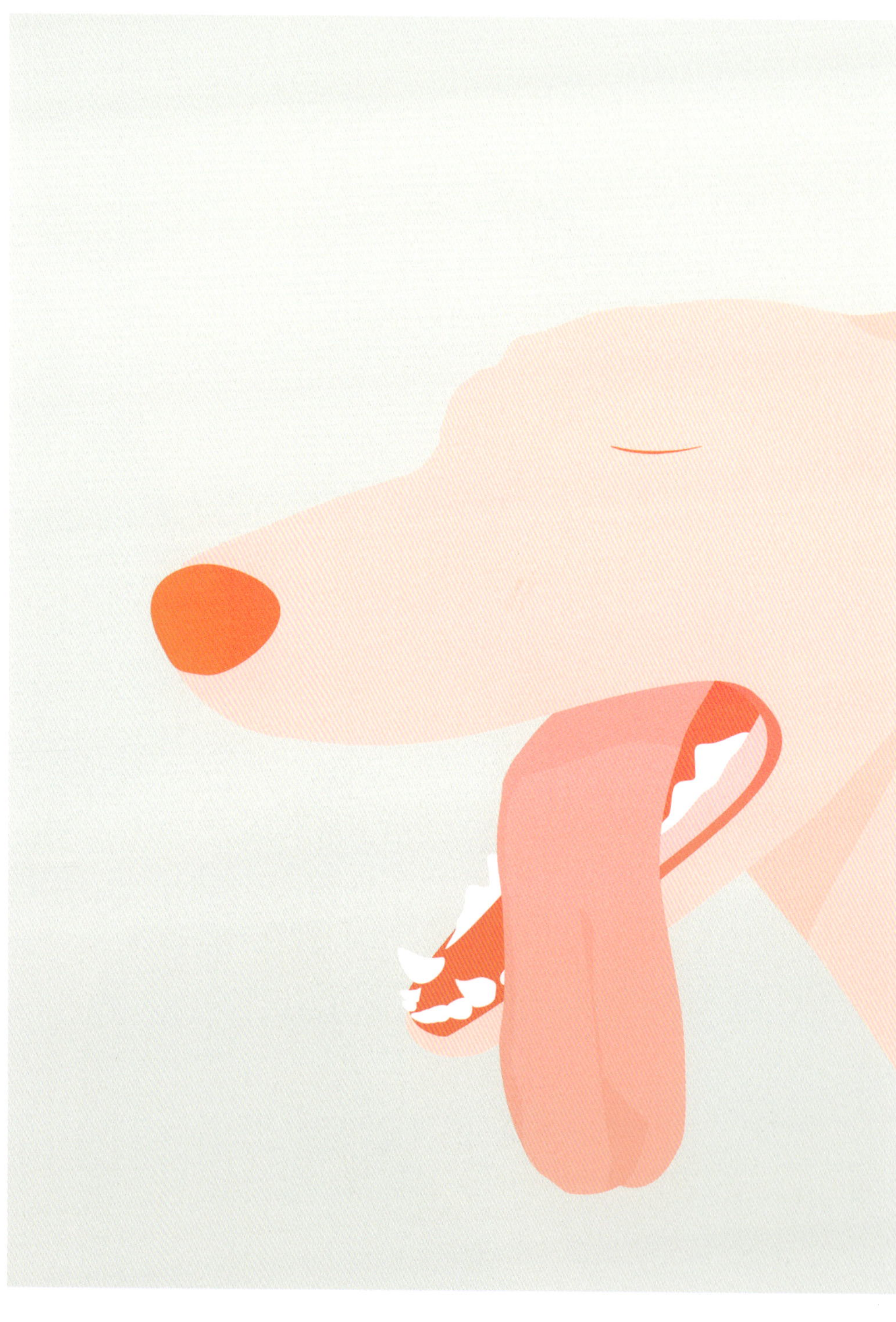

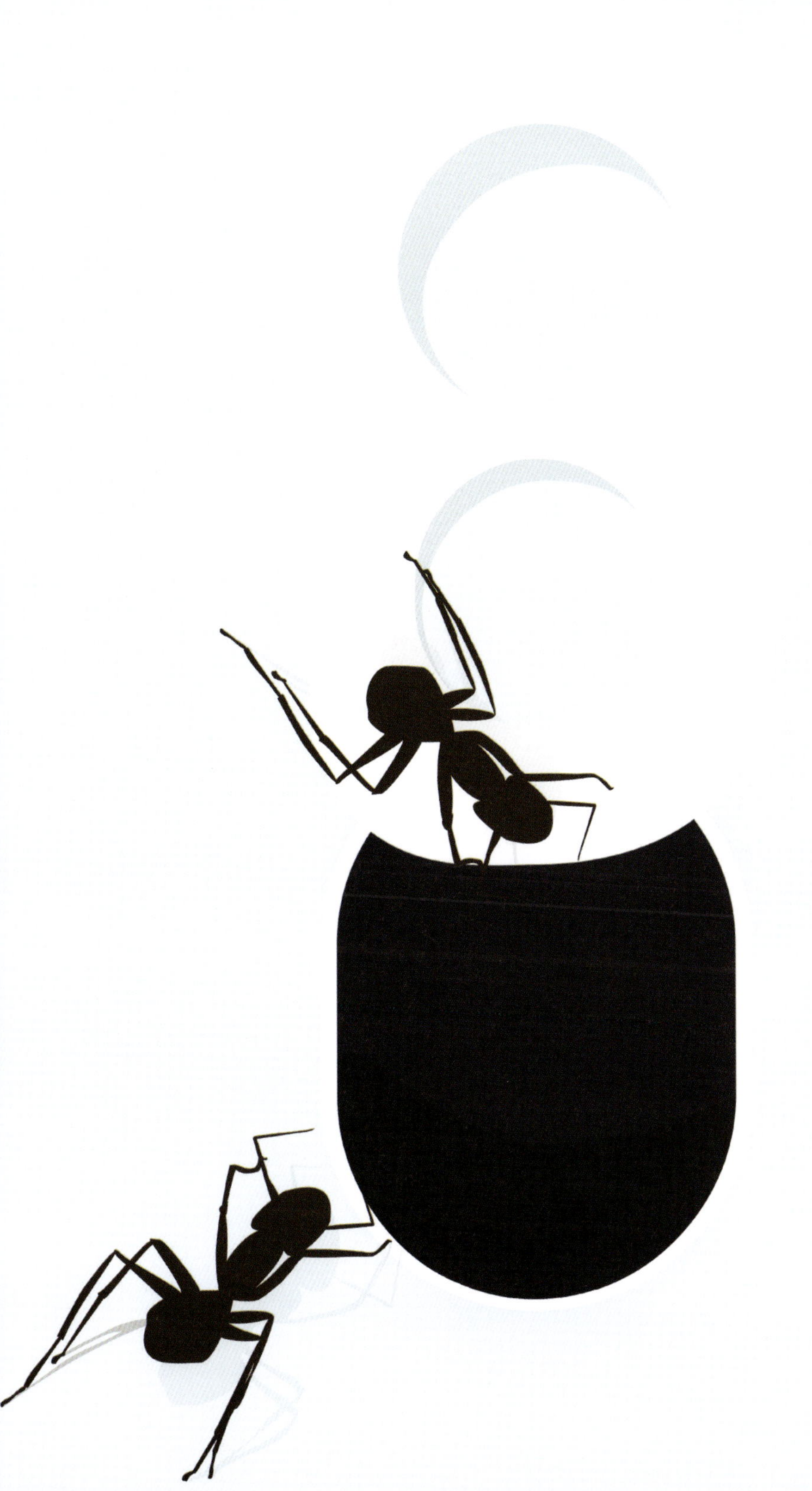

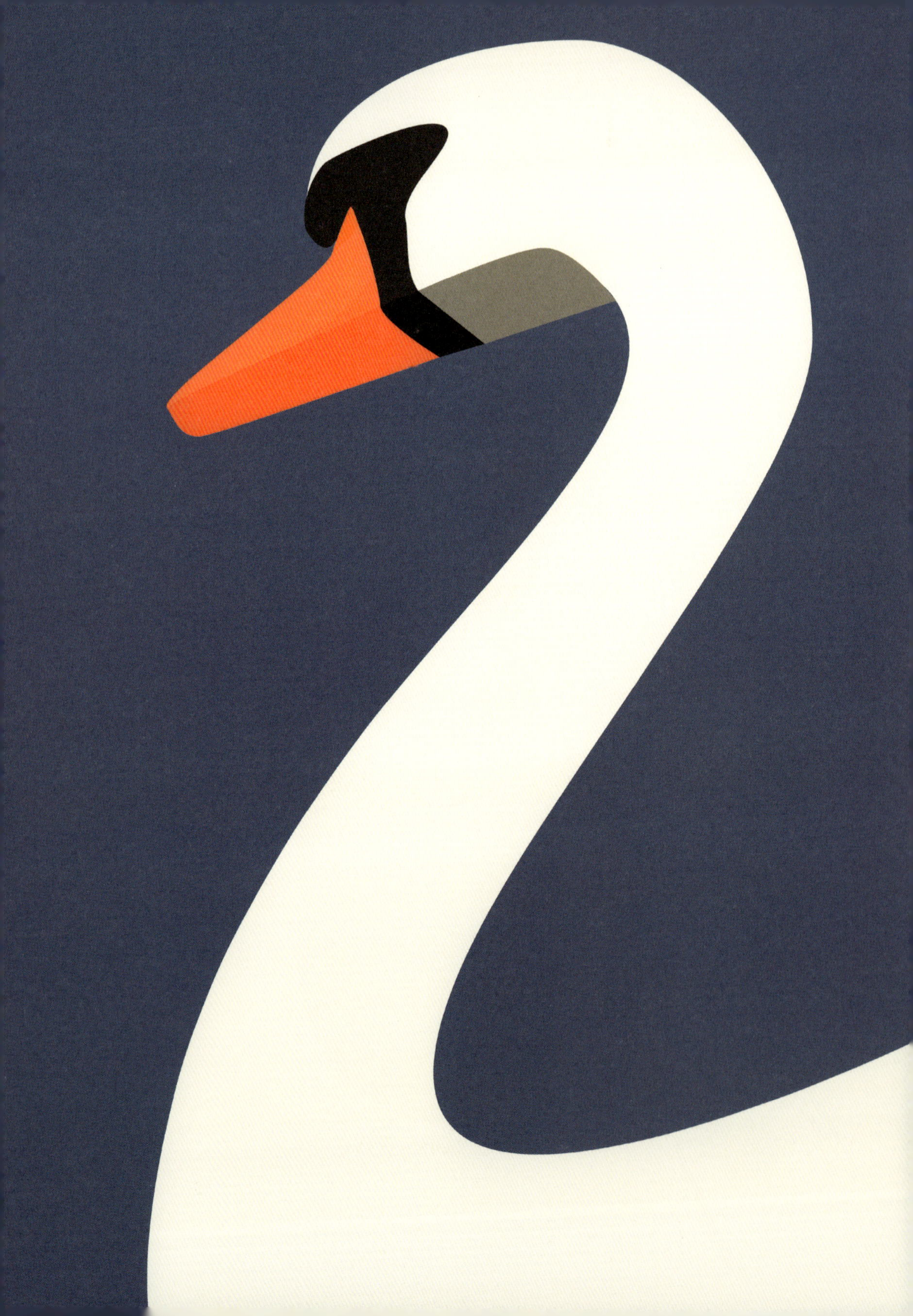

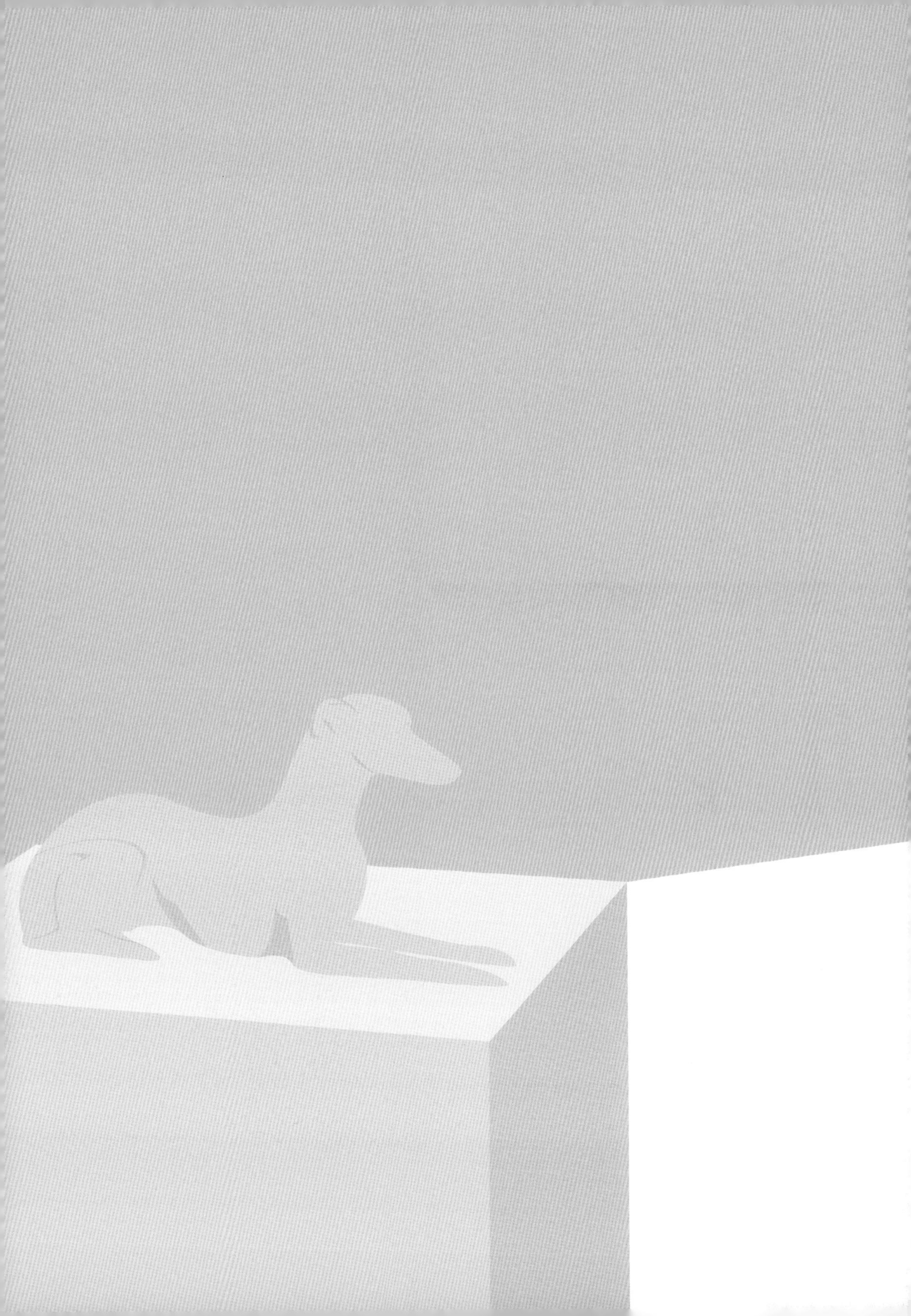

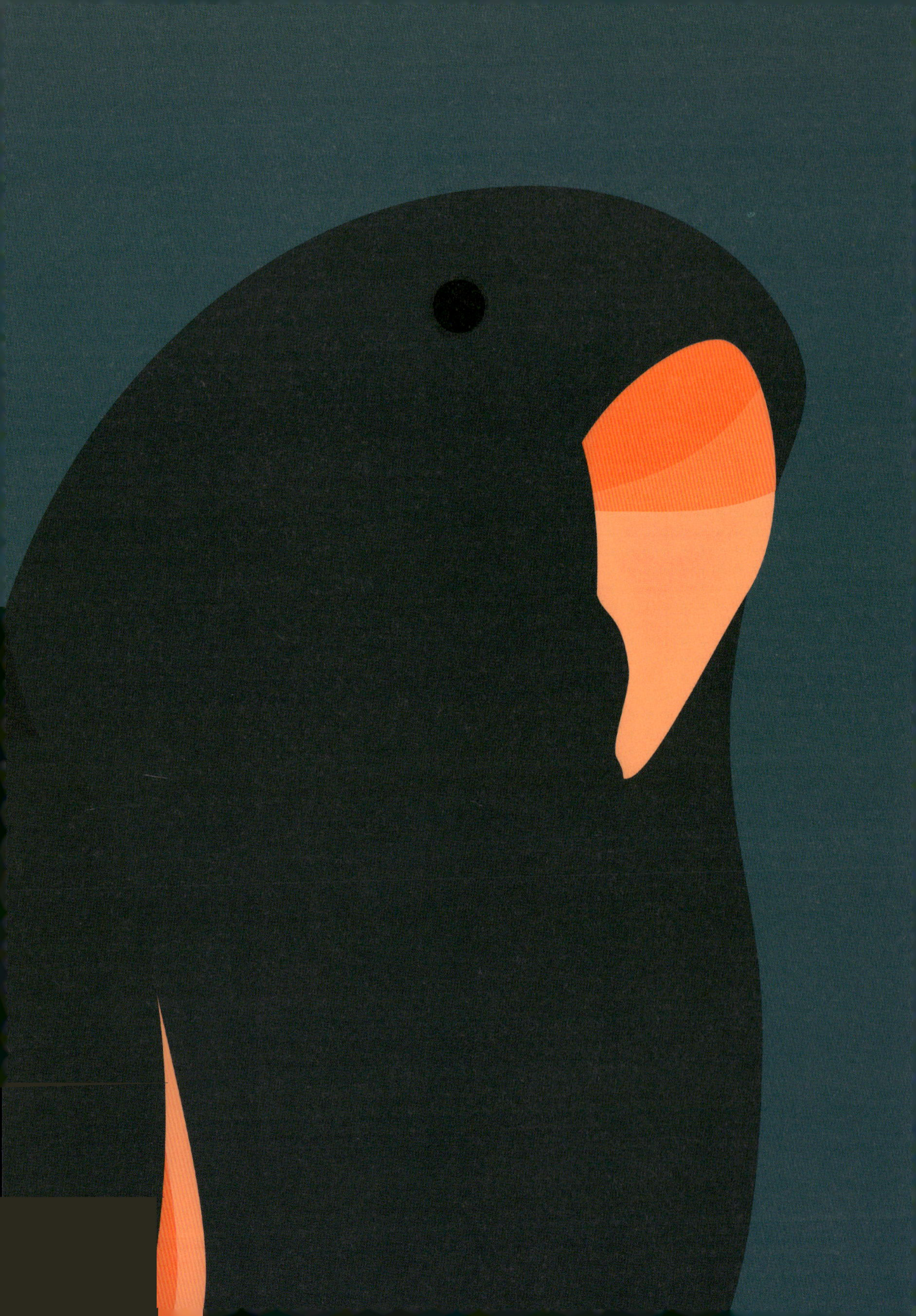

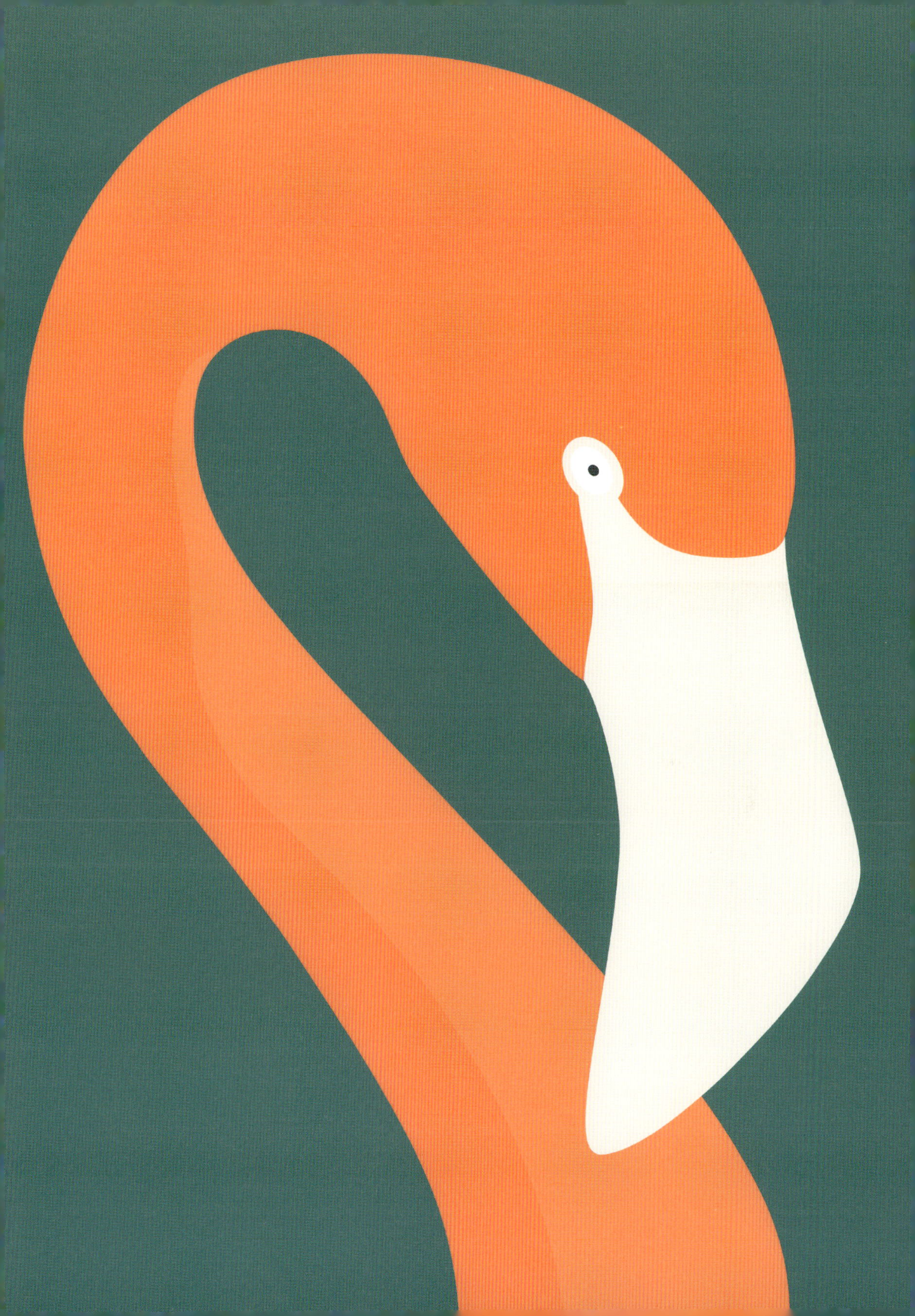

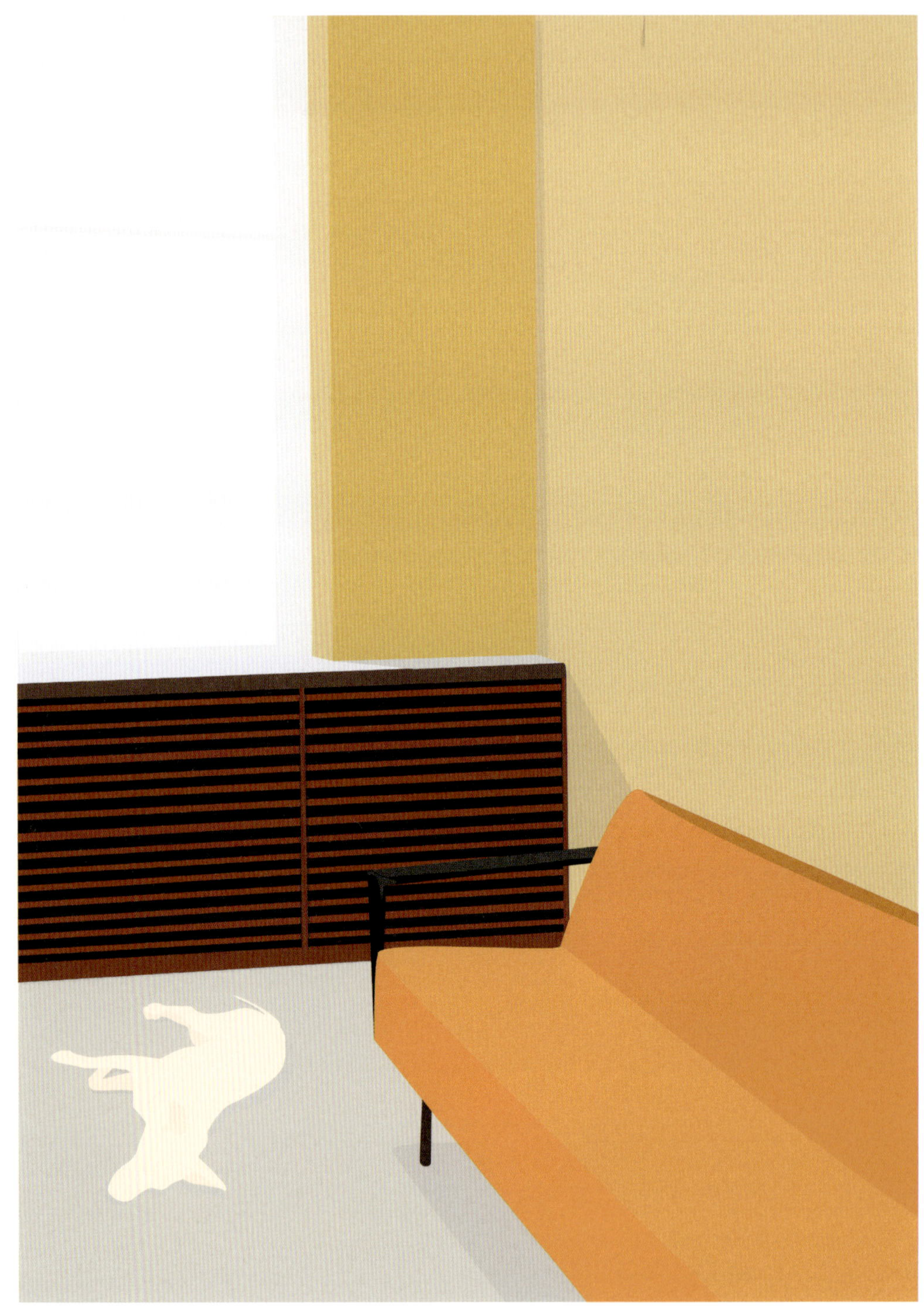

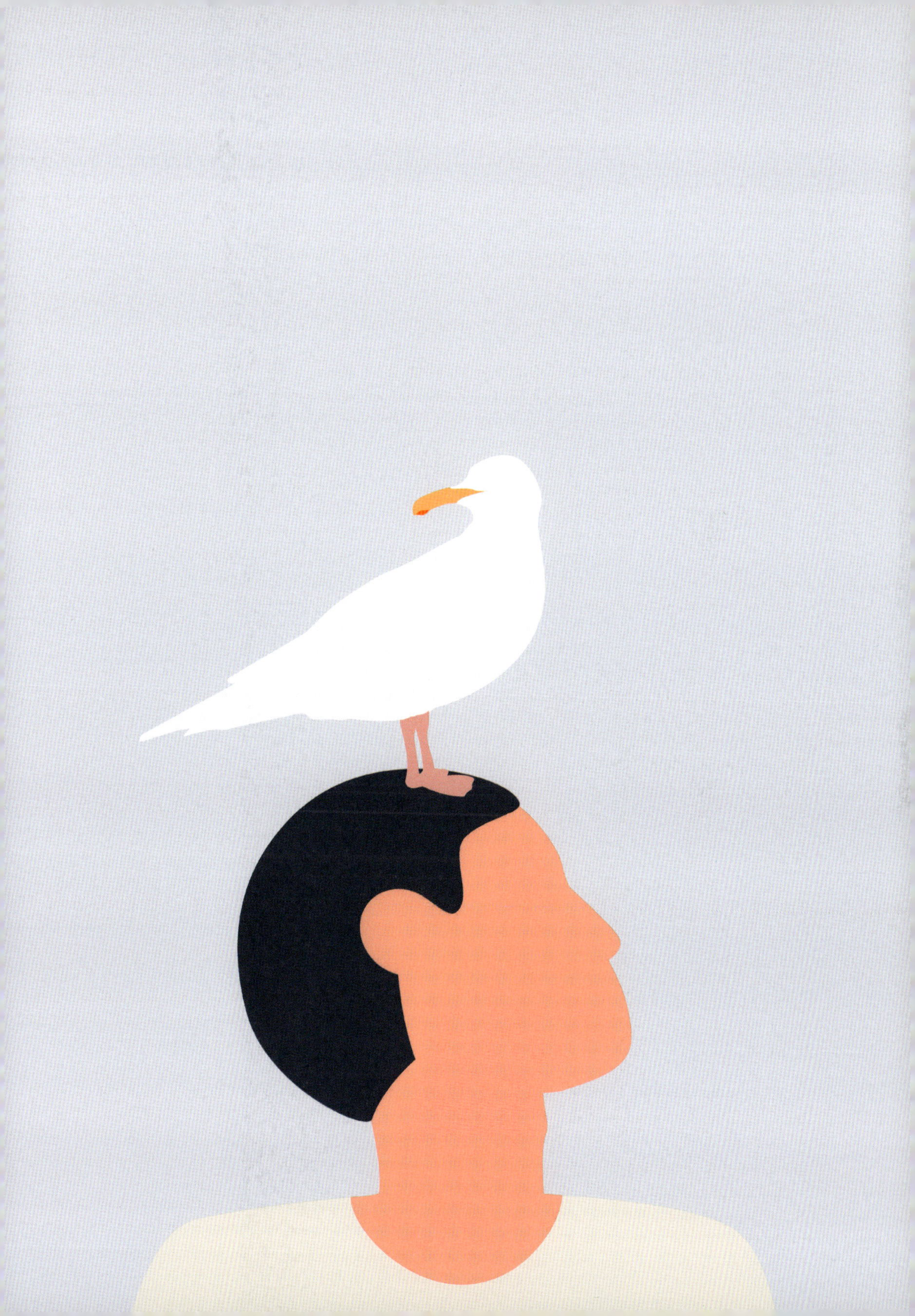

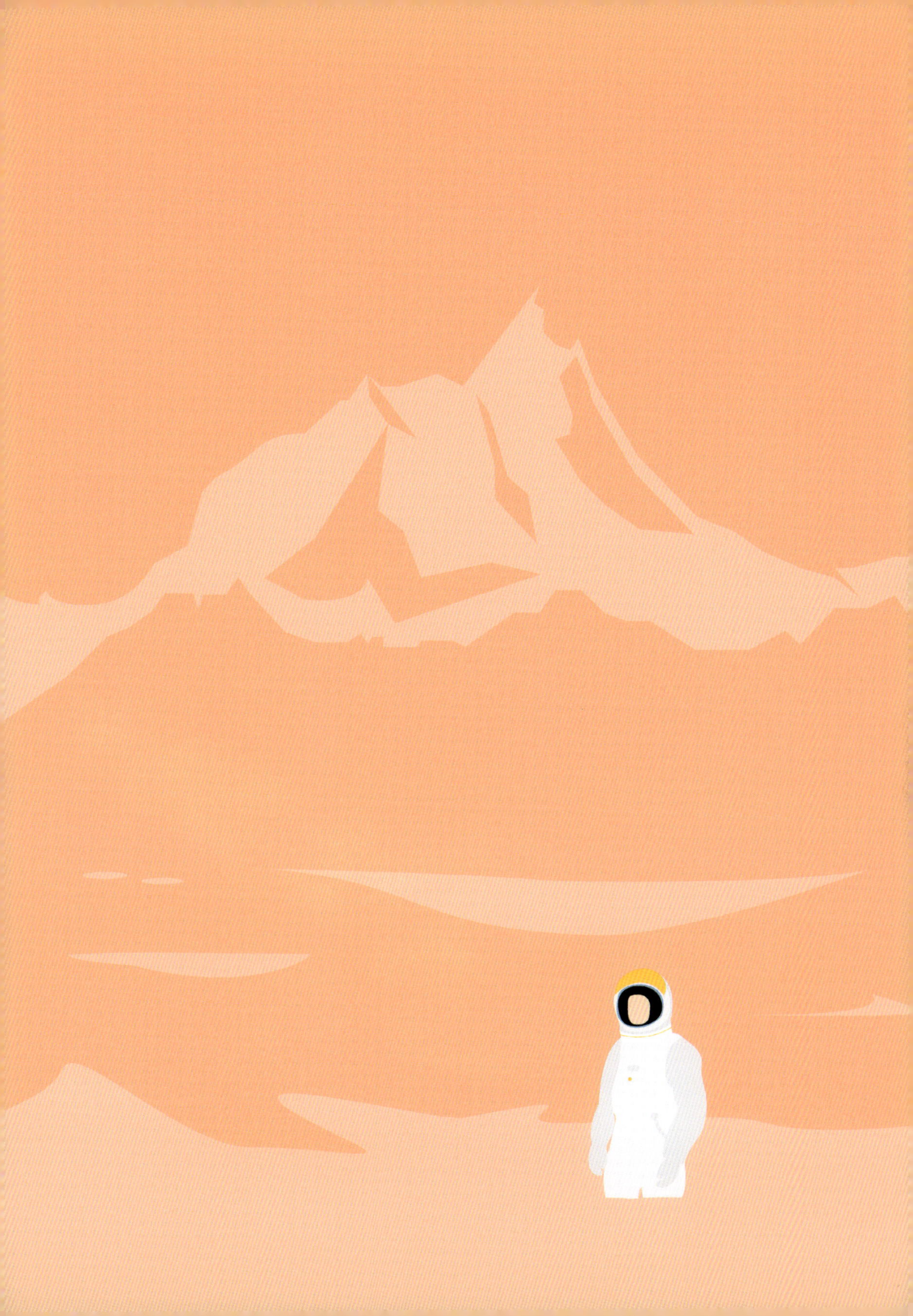

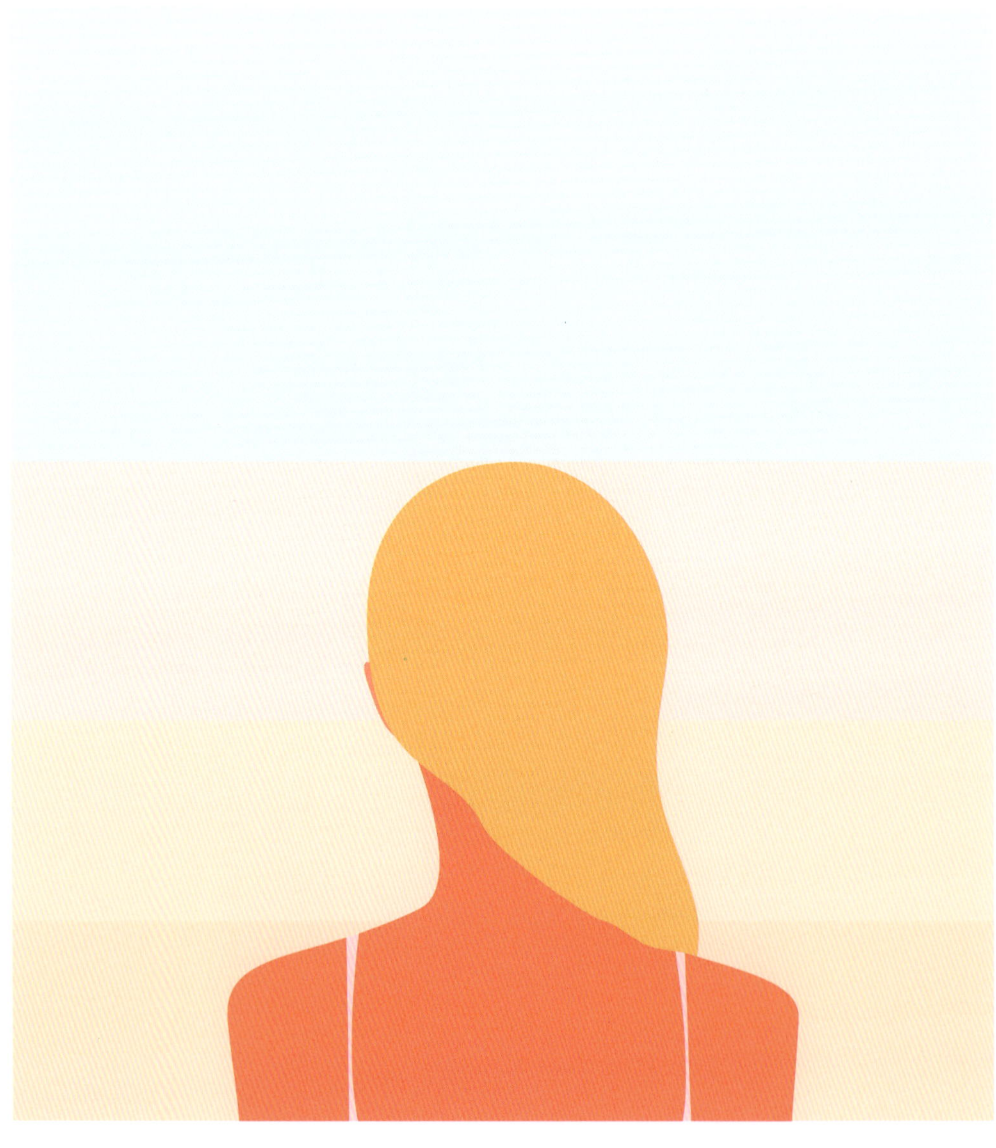

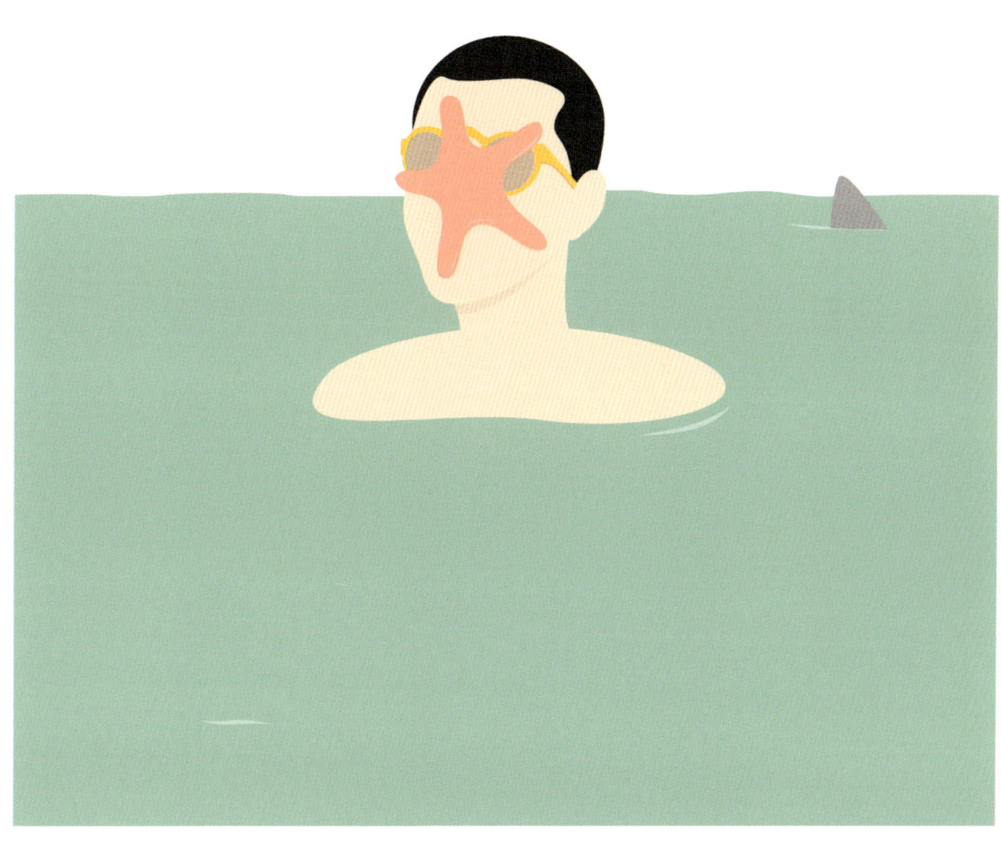

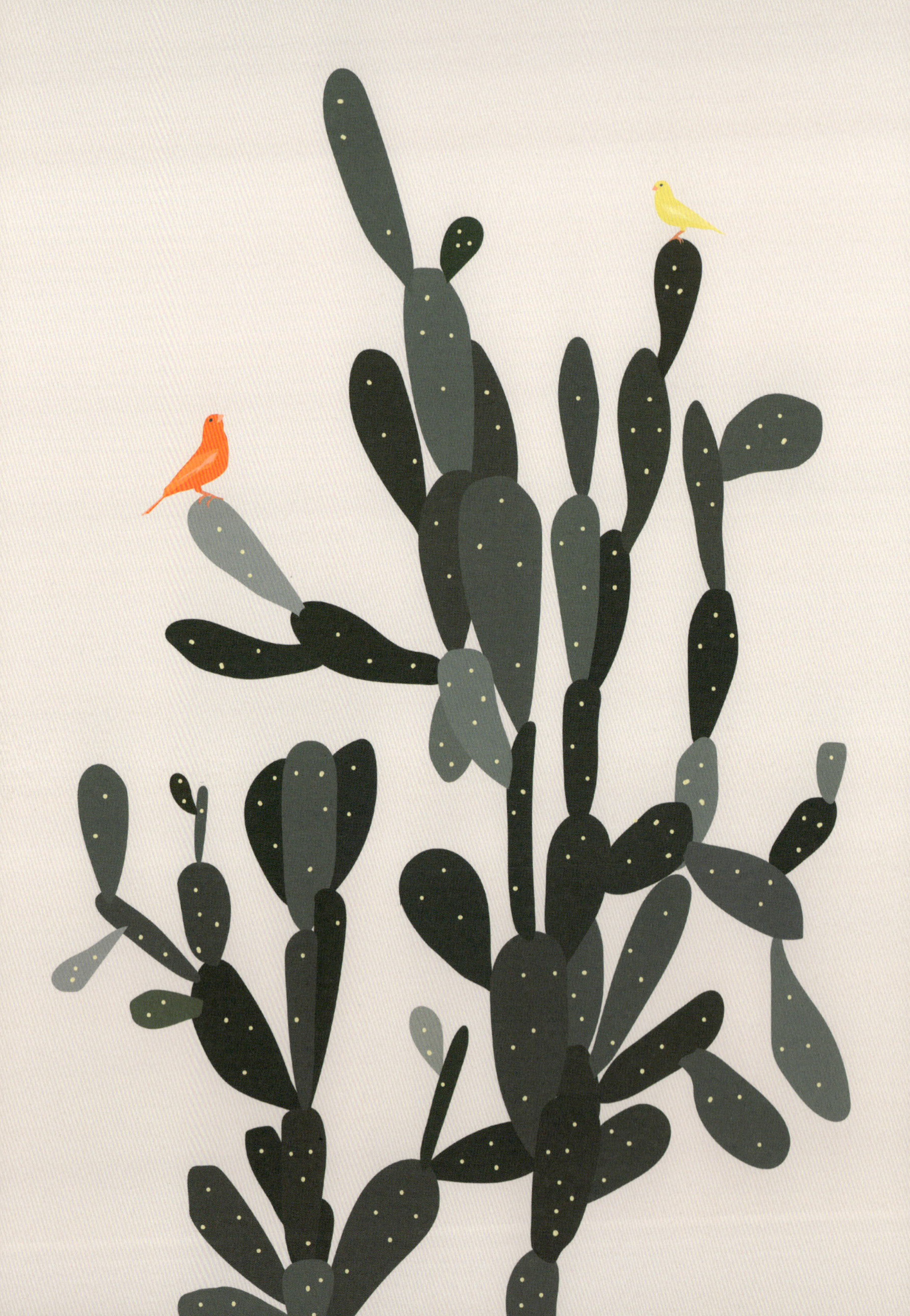

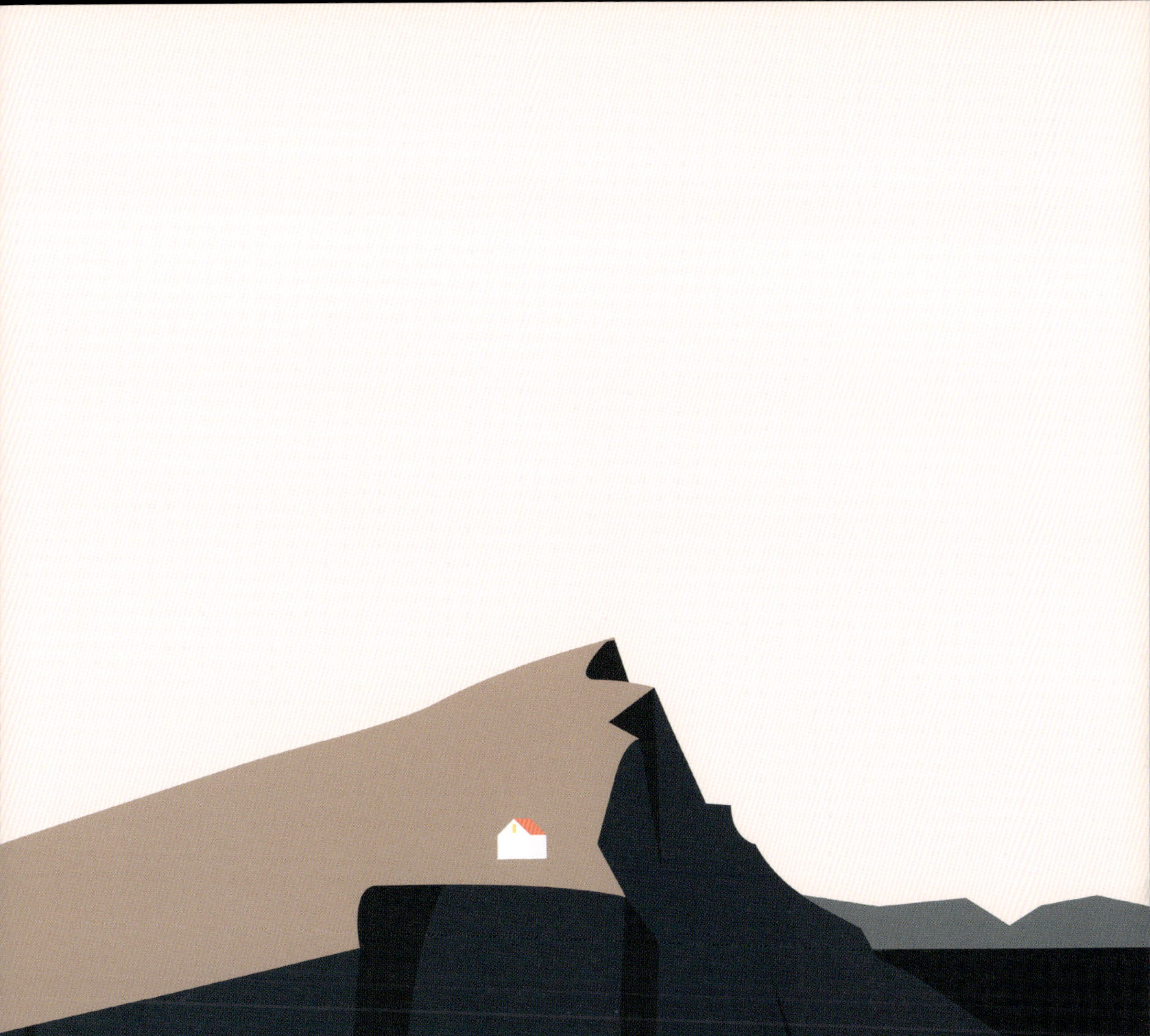

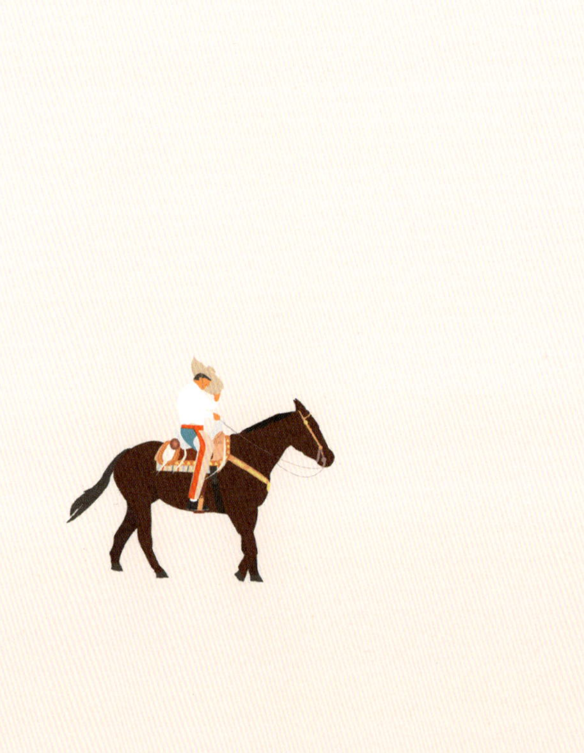

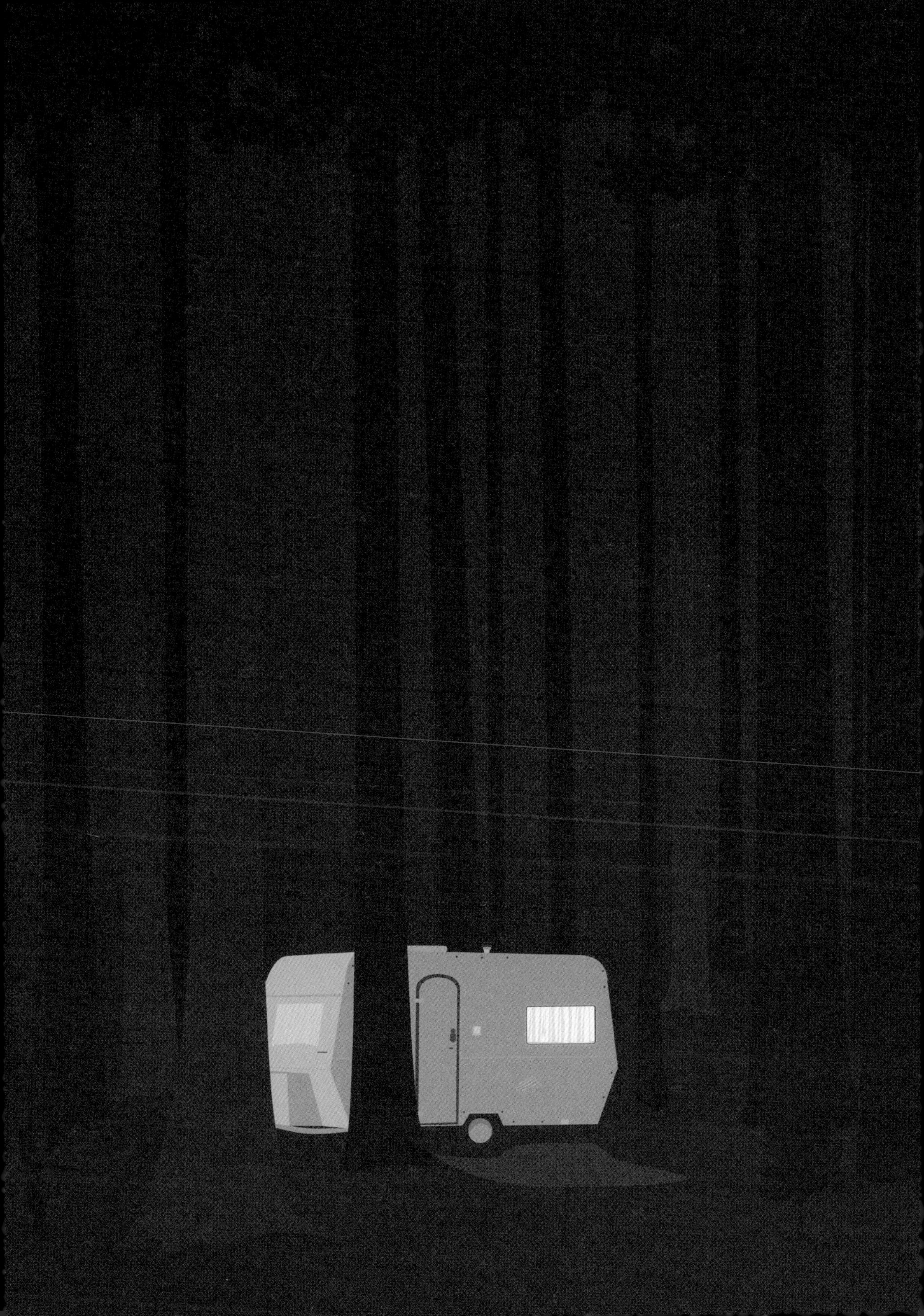

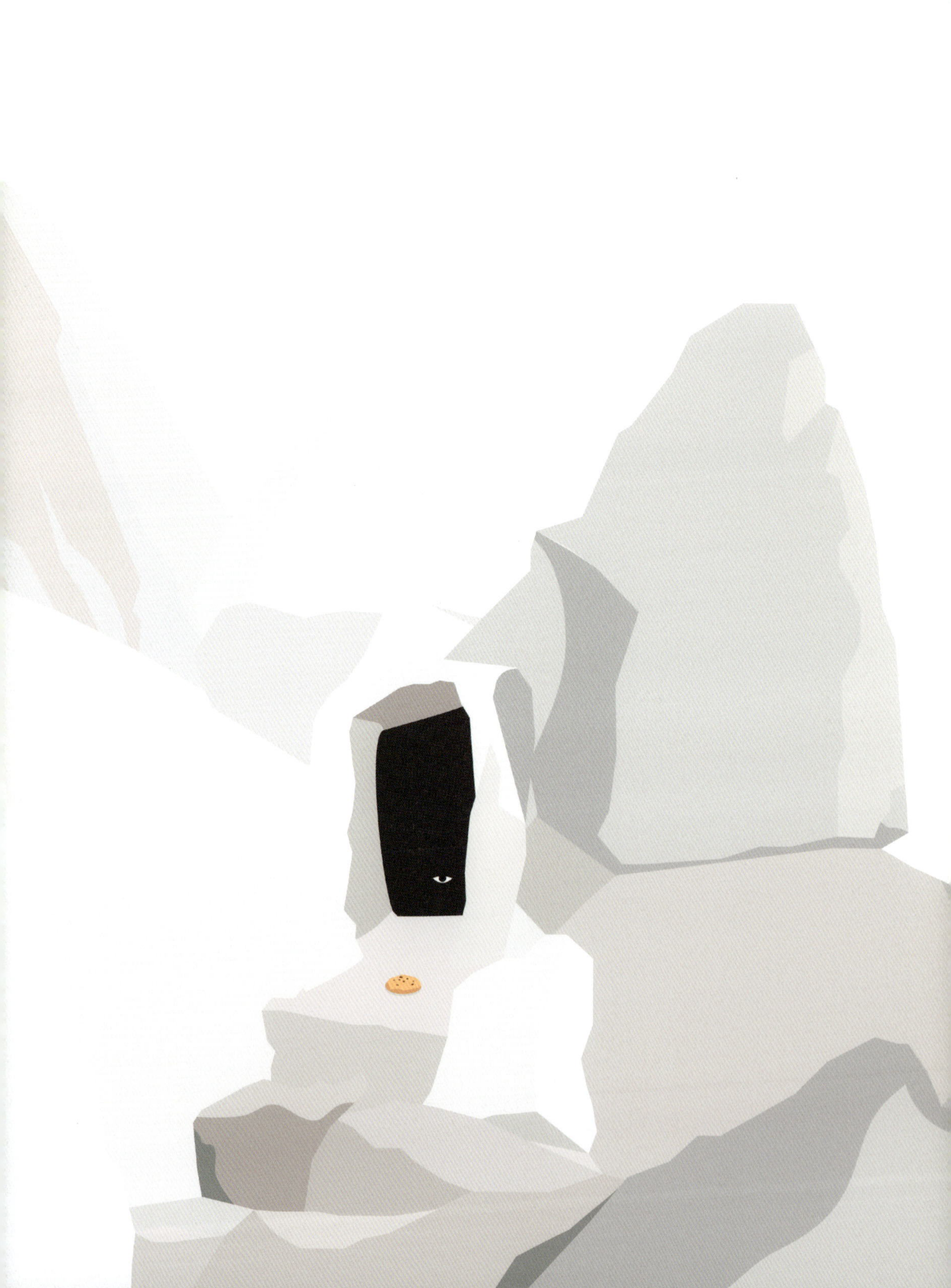

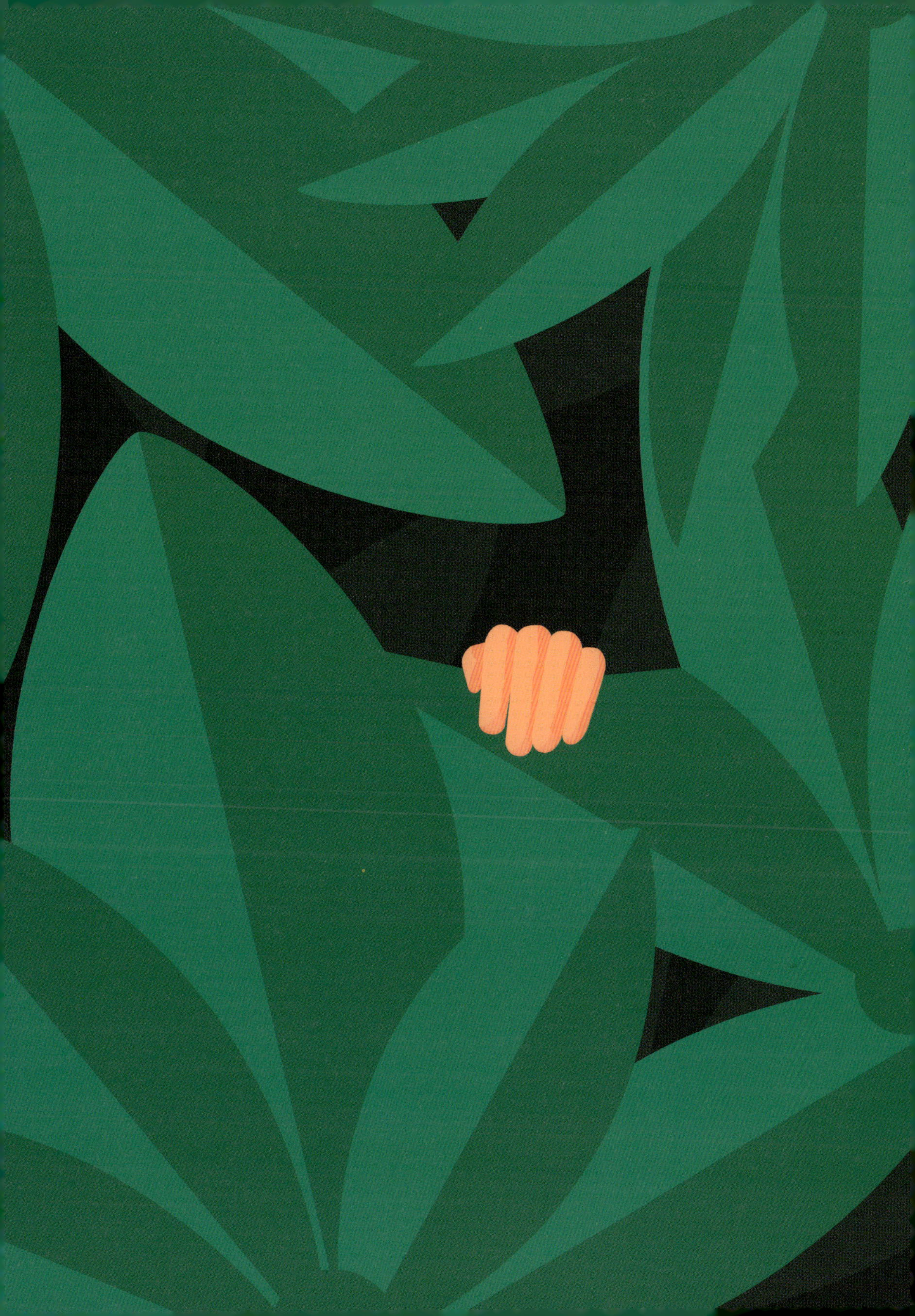

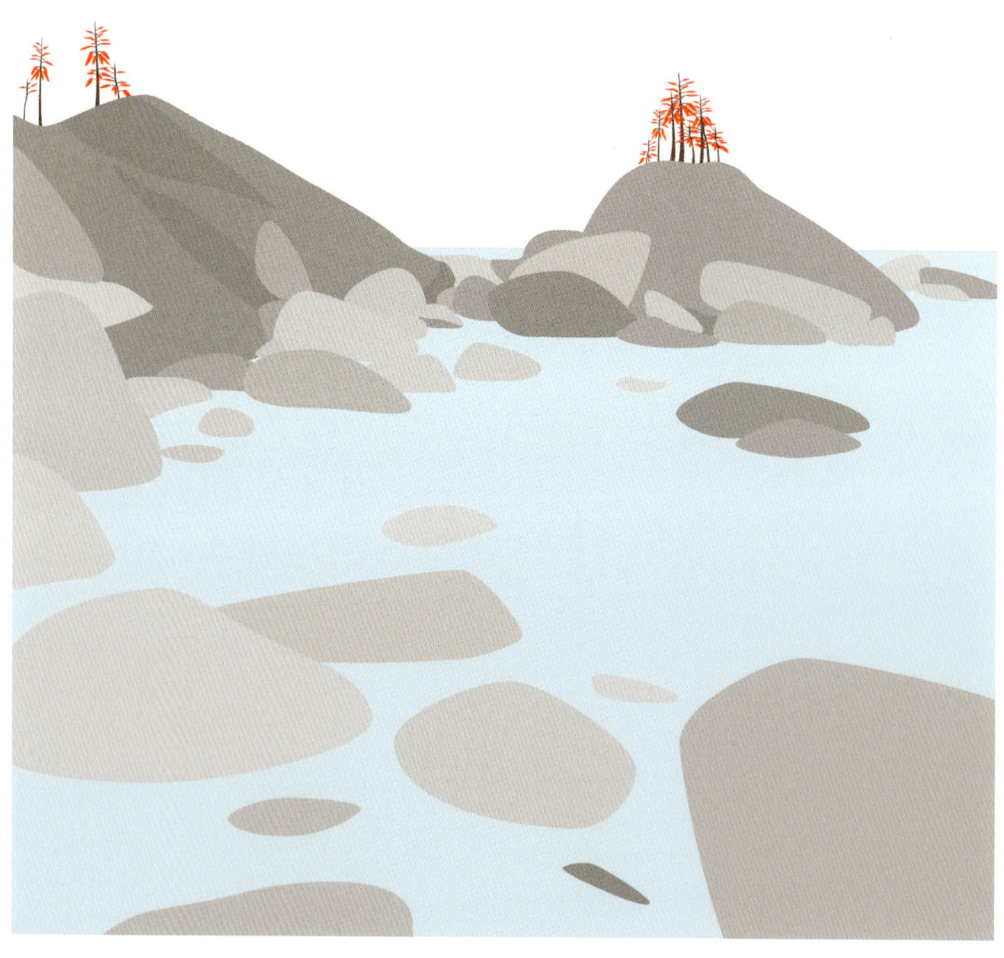

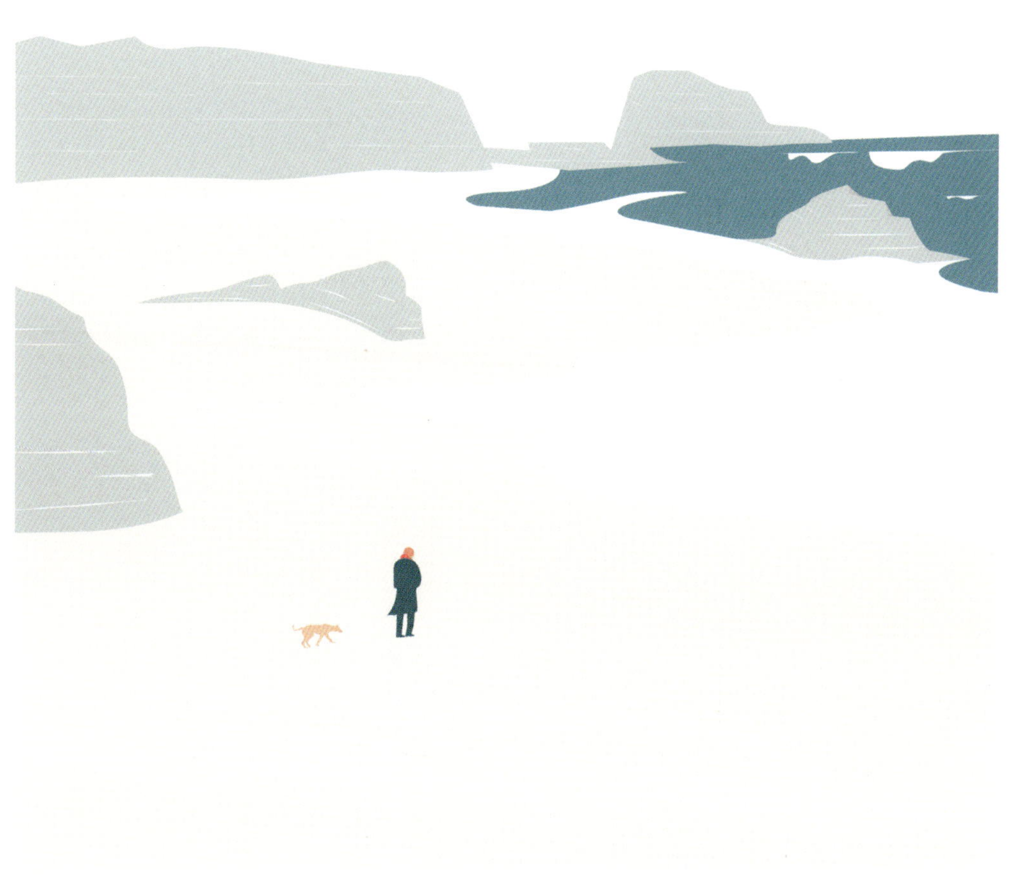

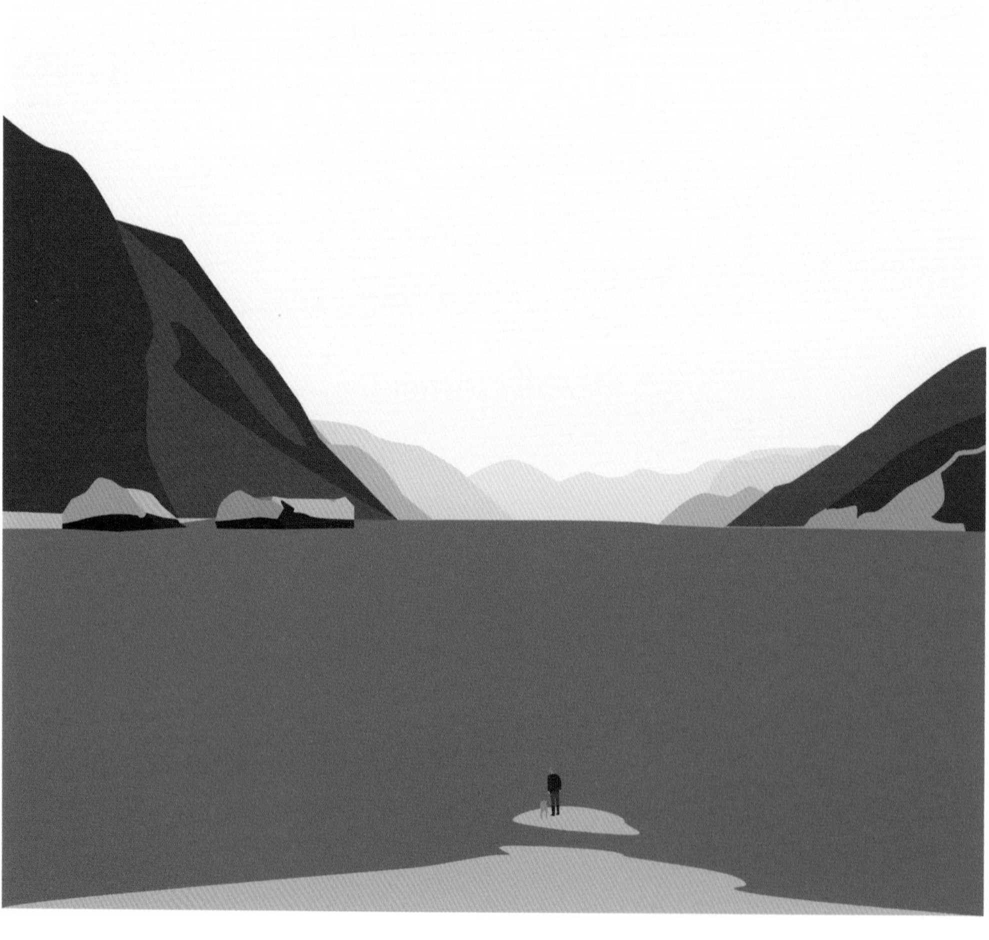

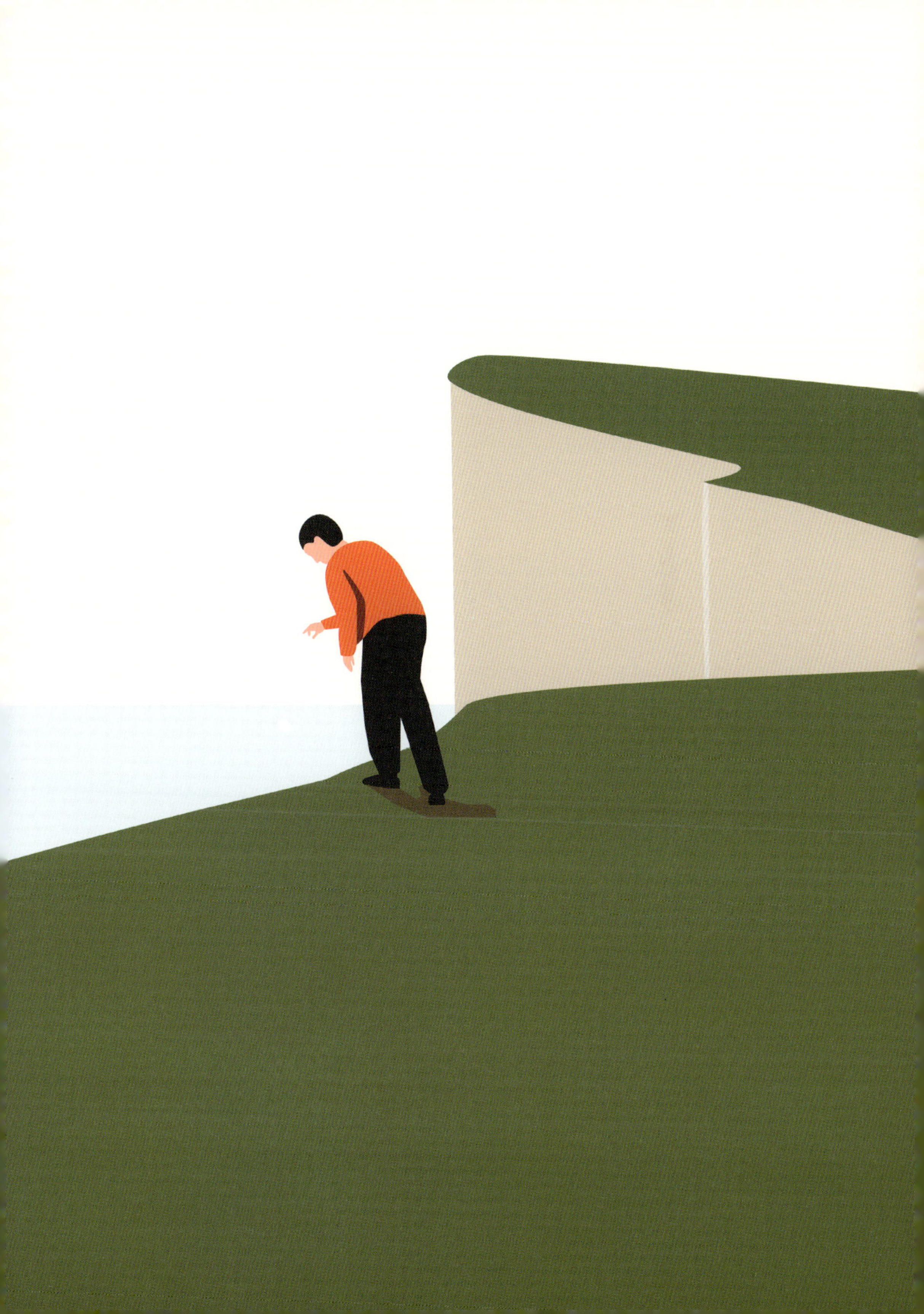

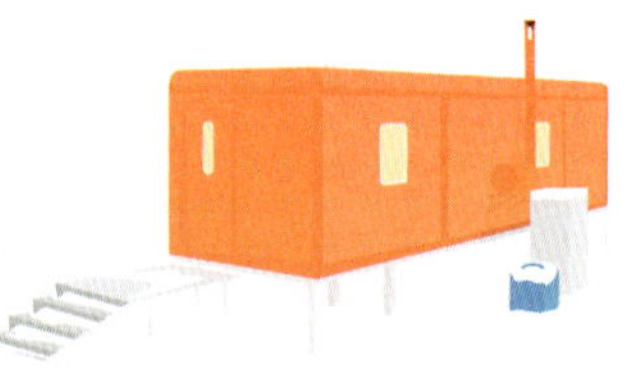

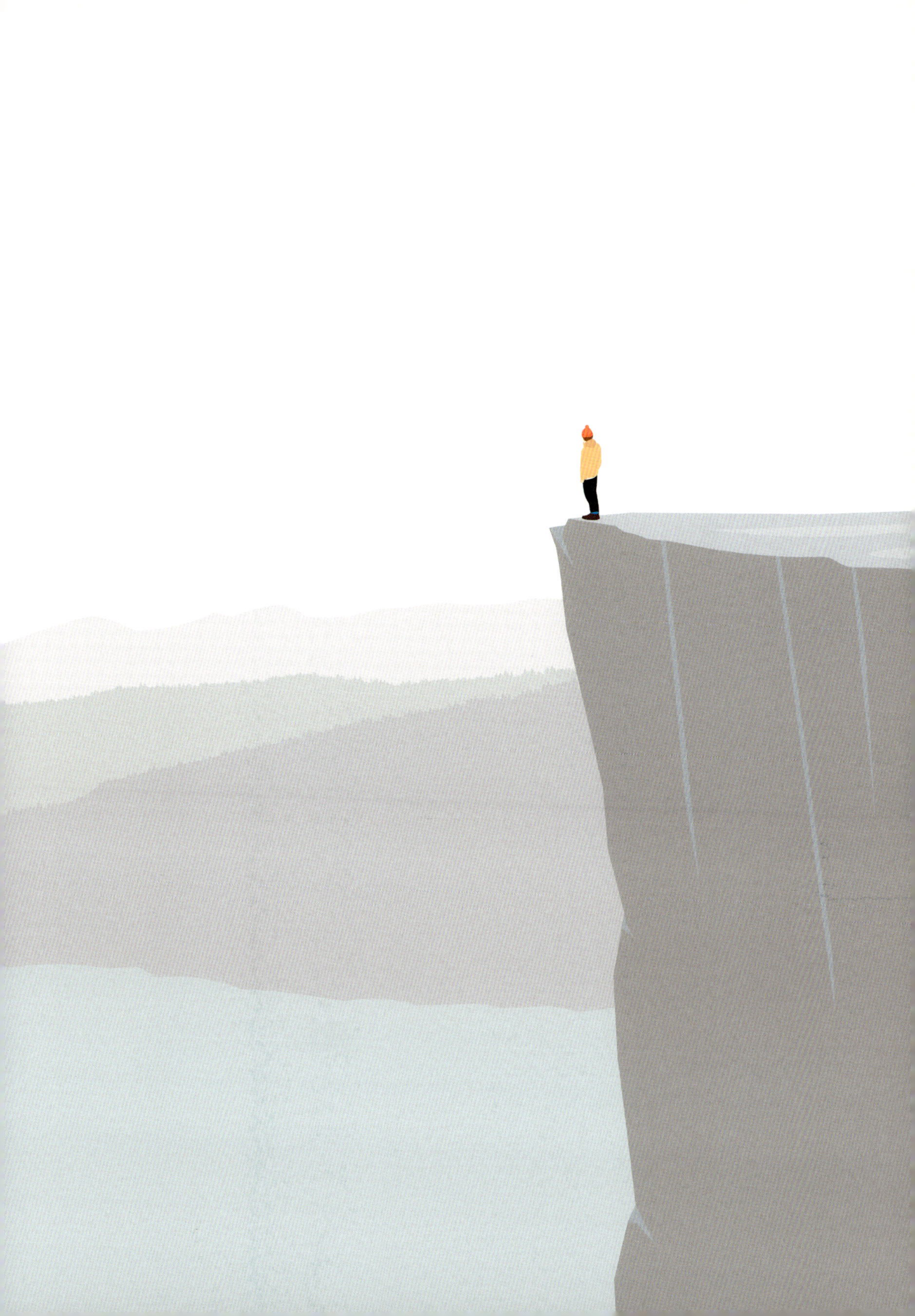

Transportation

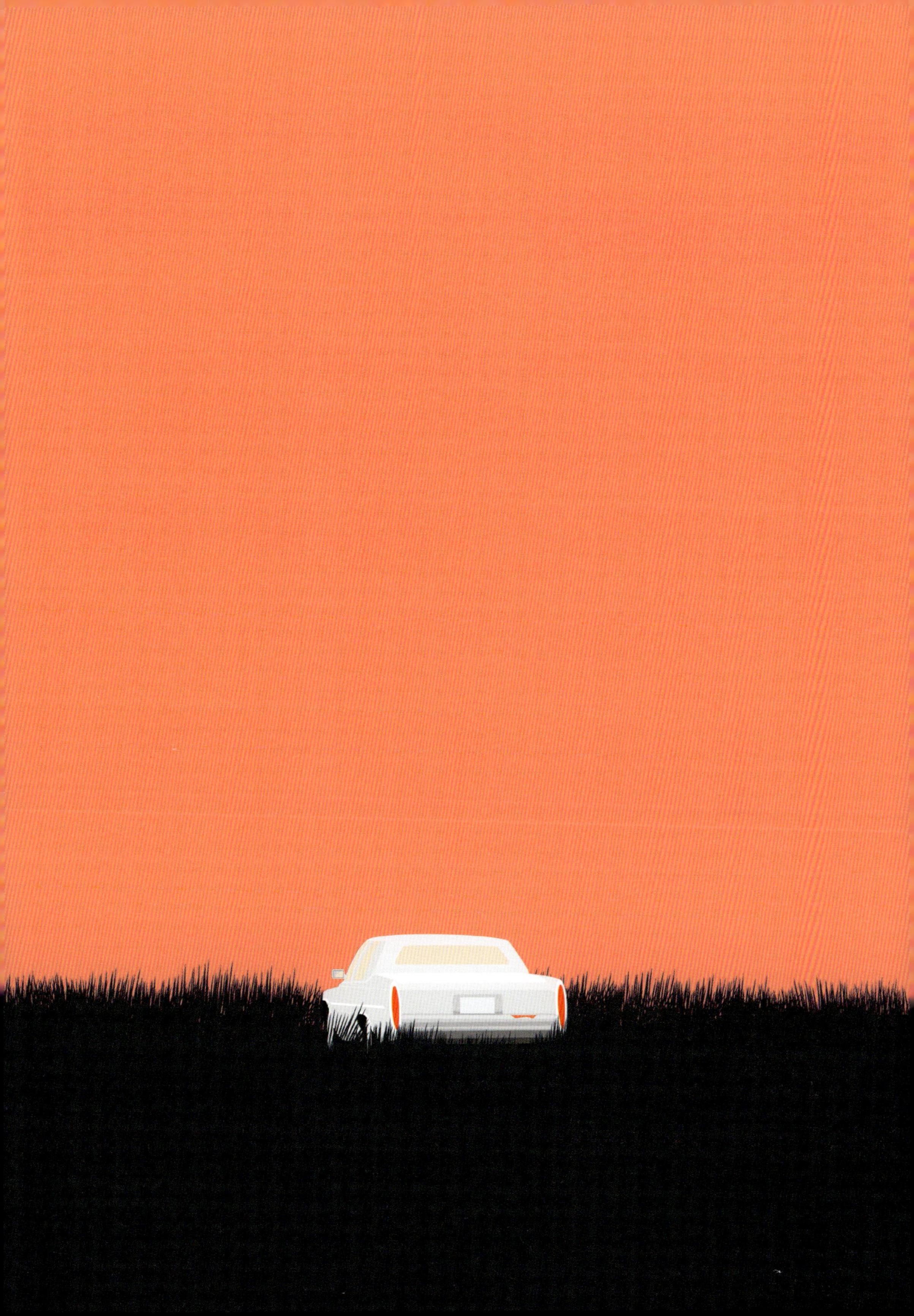

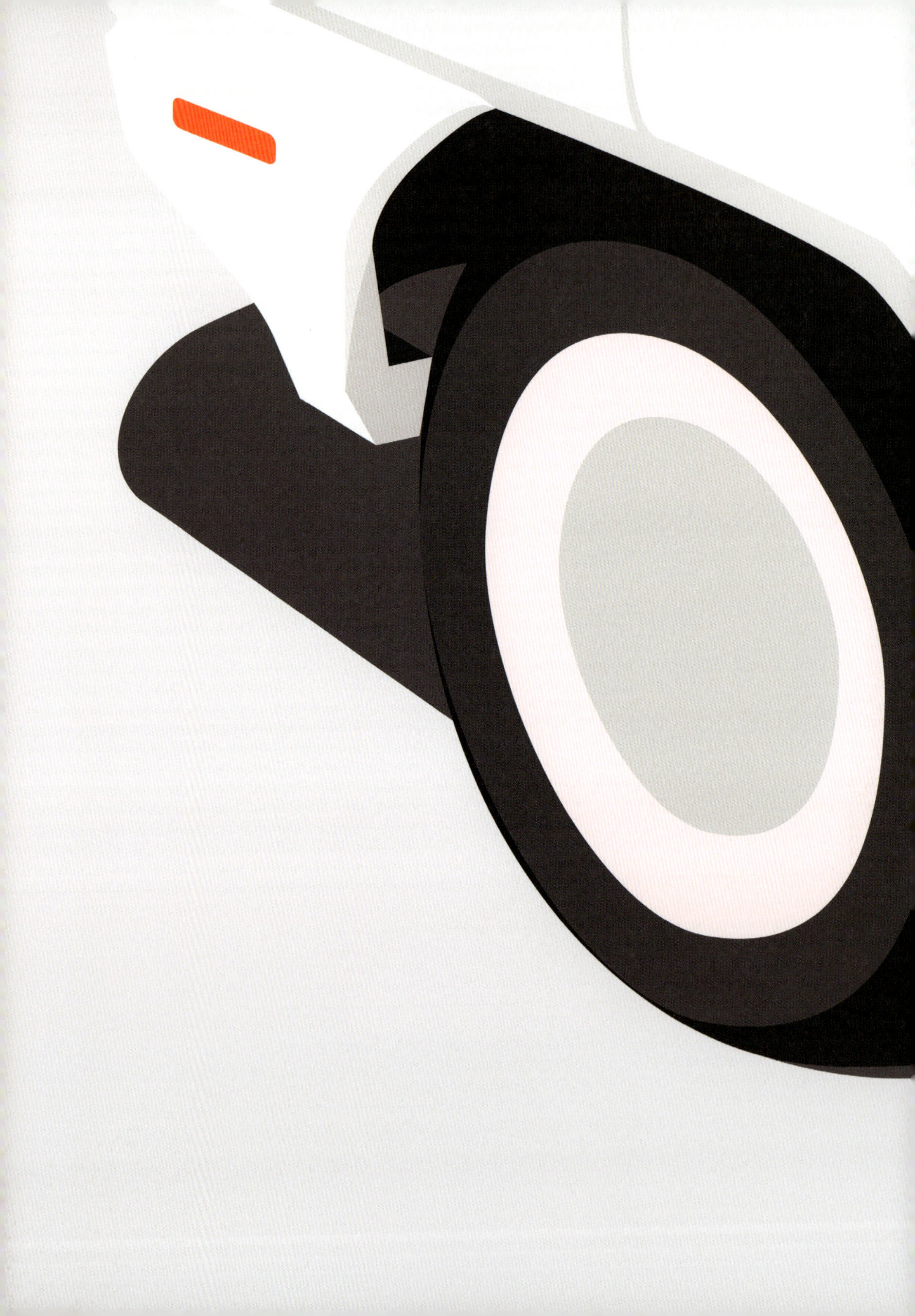

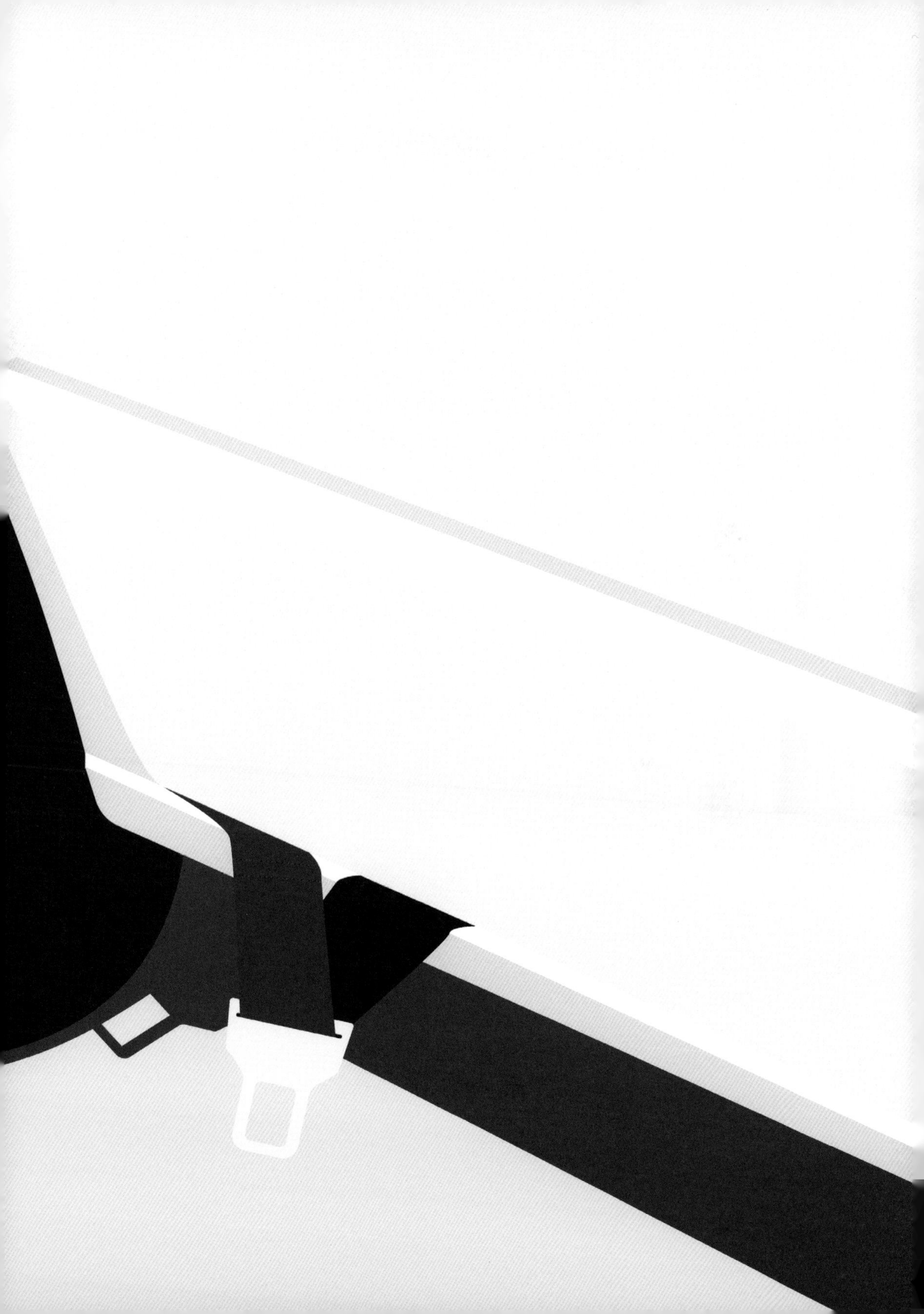

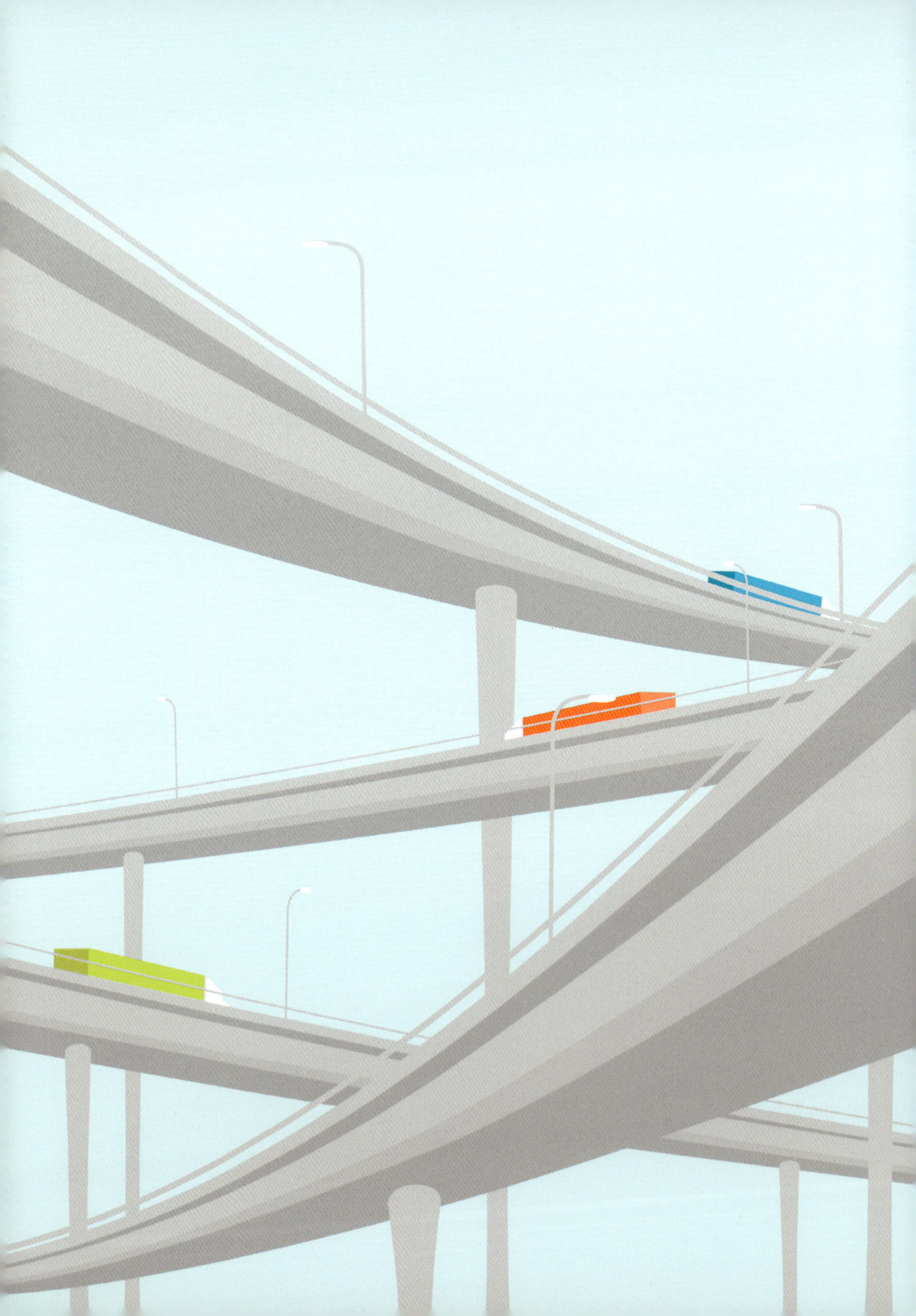

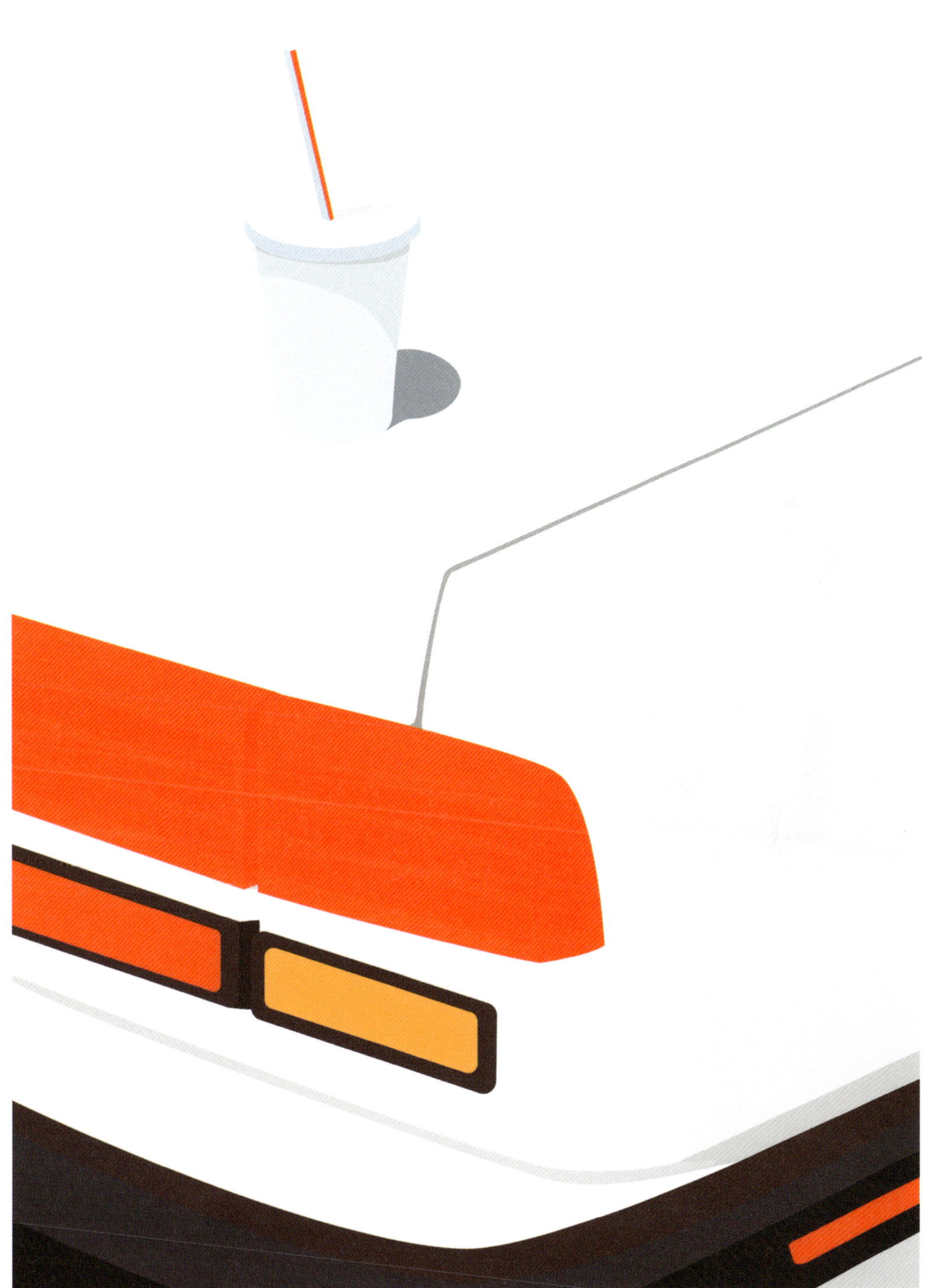

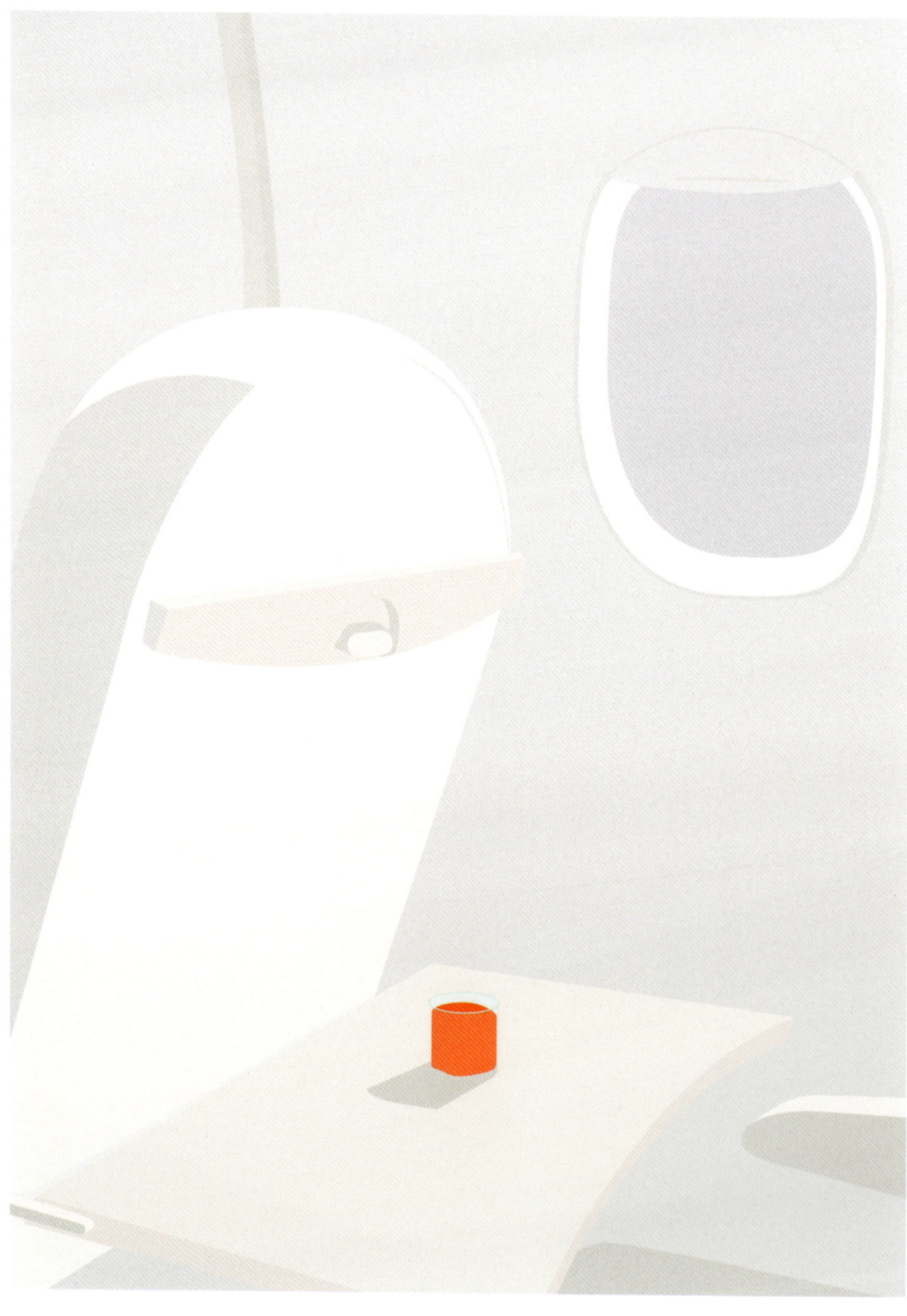

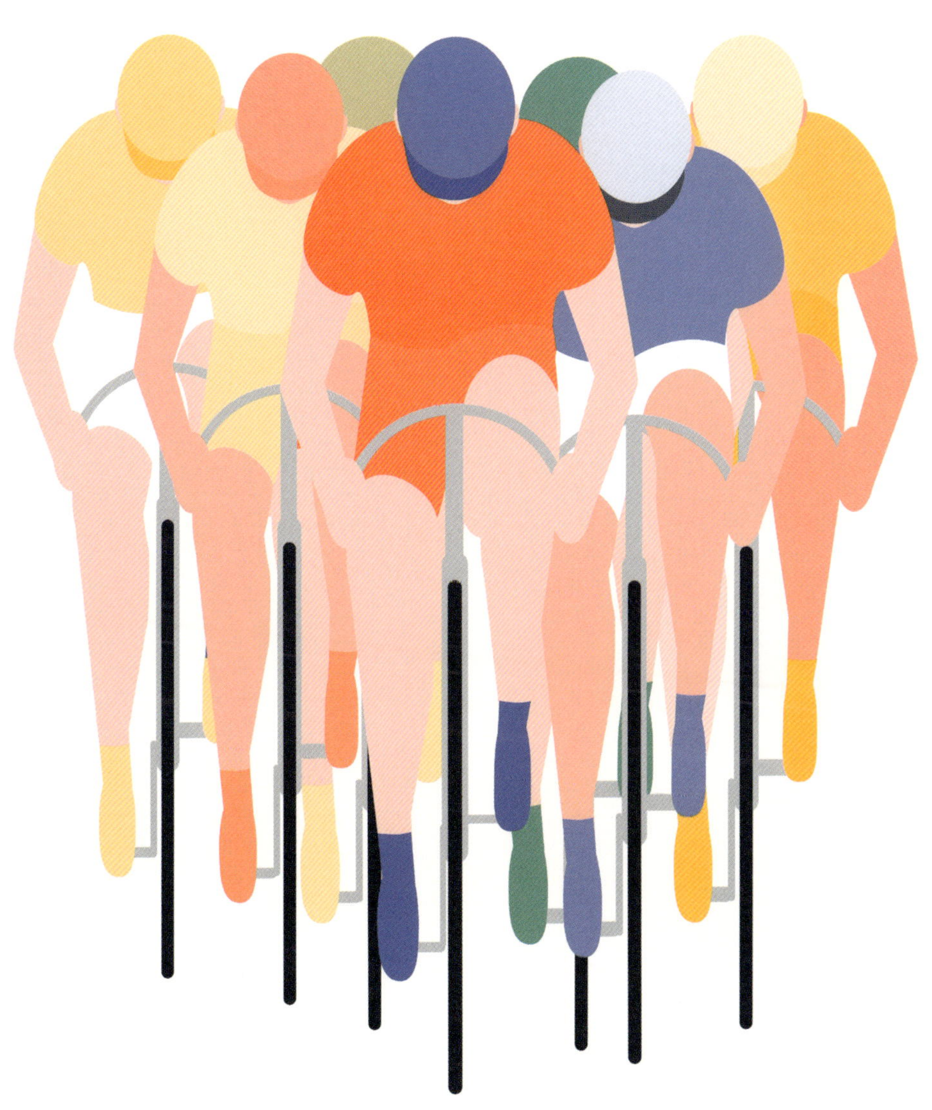

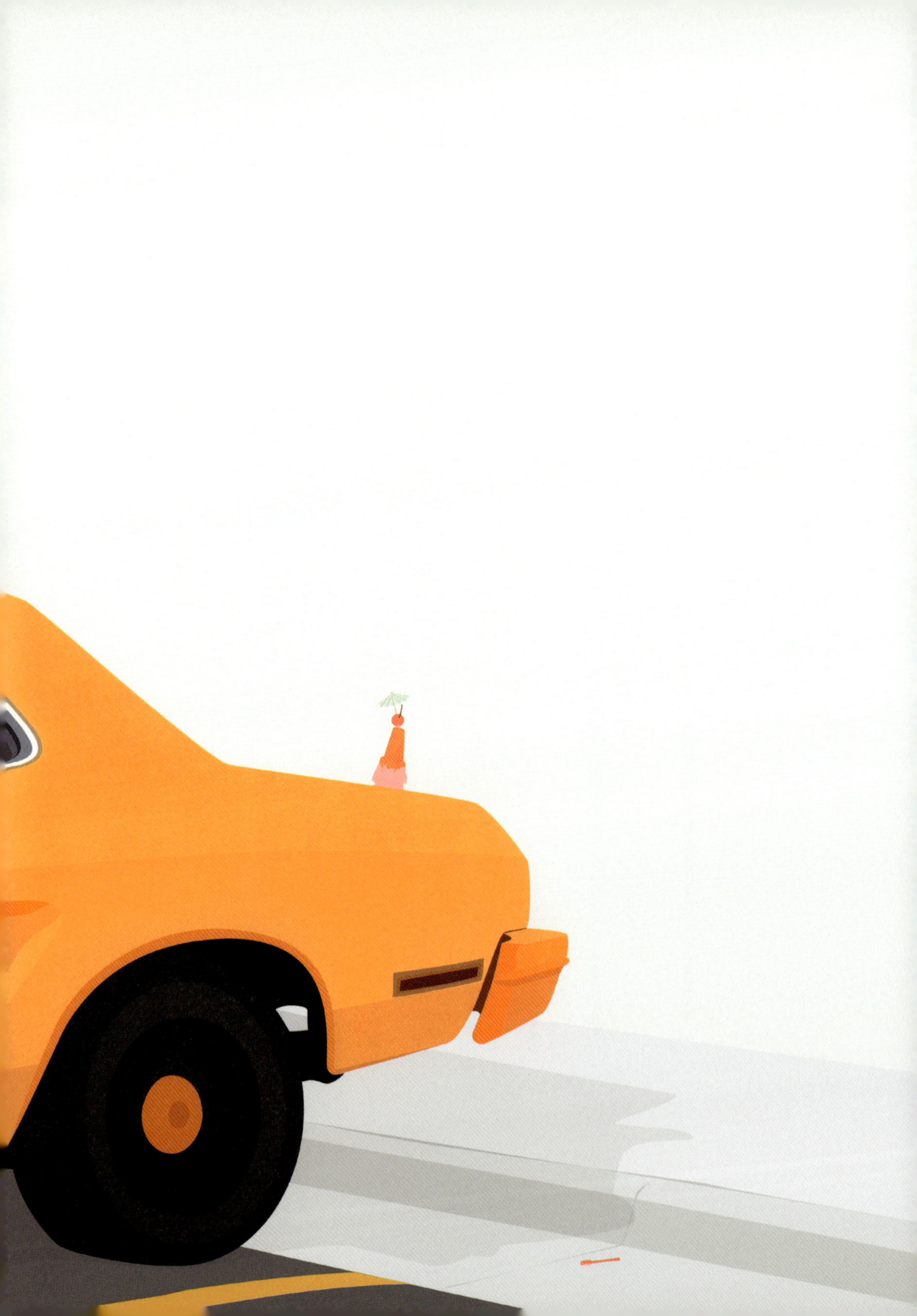

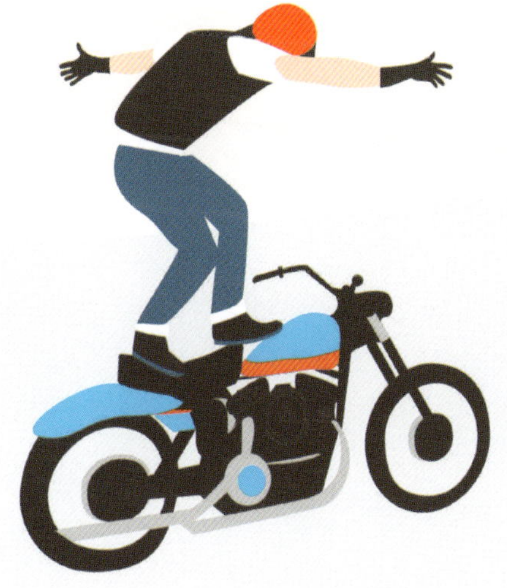

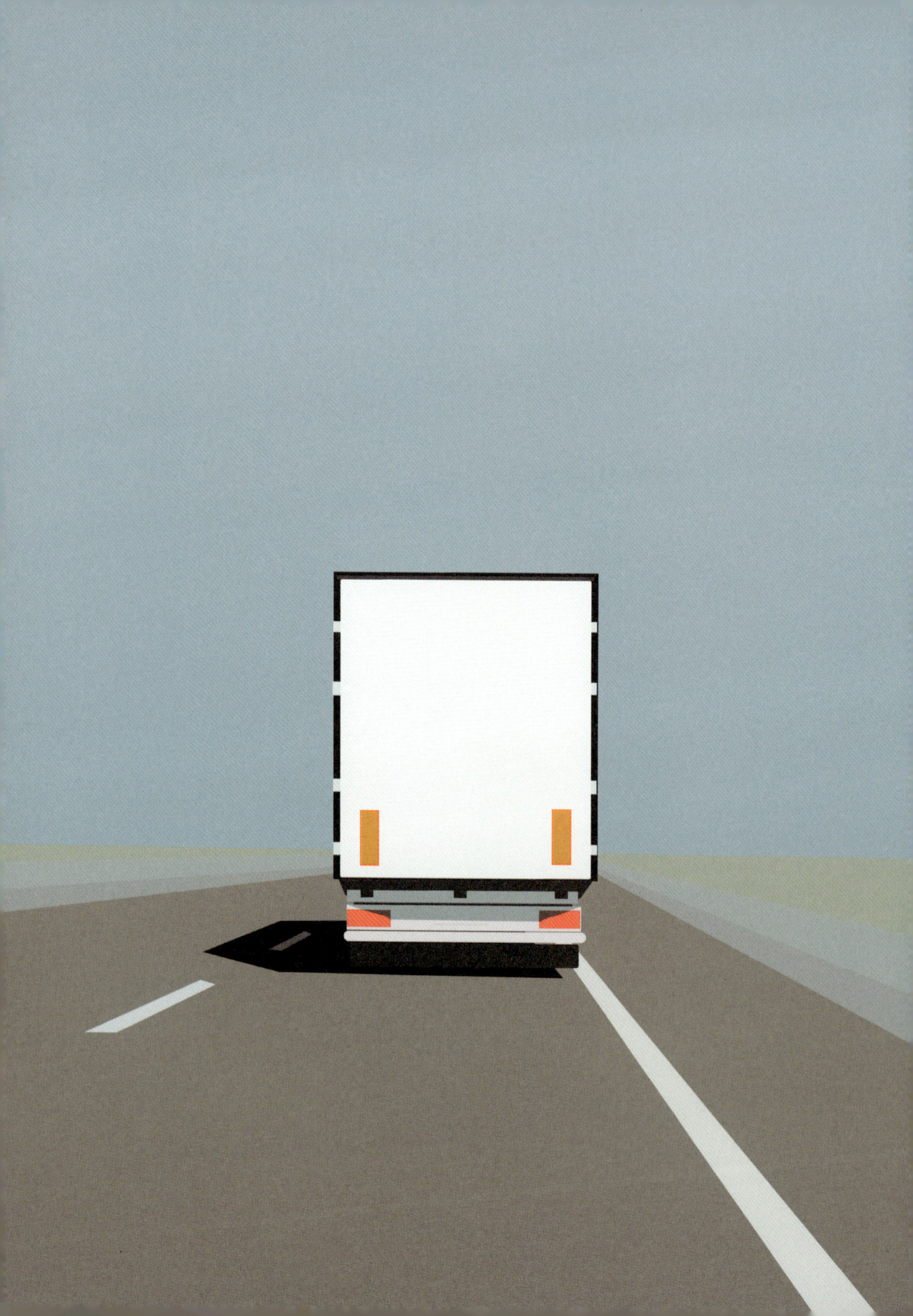

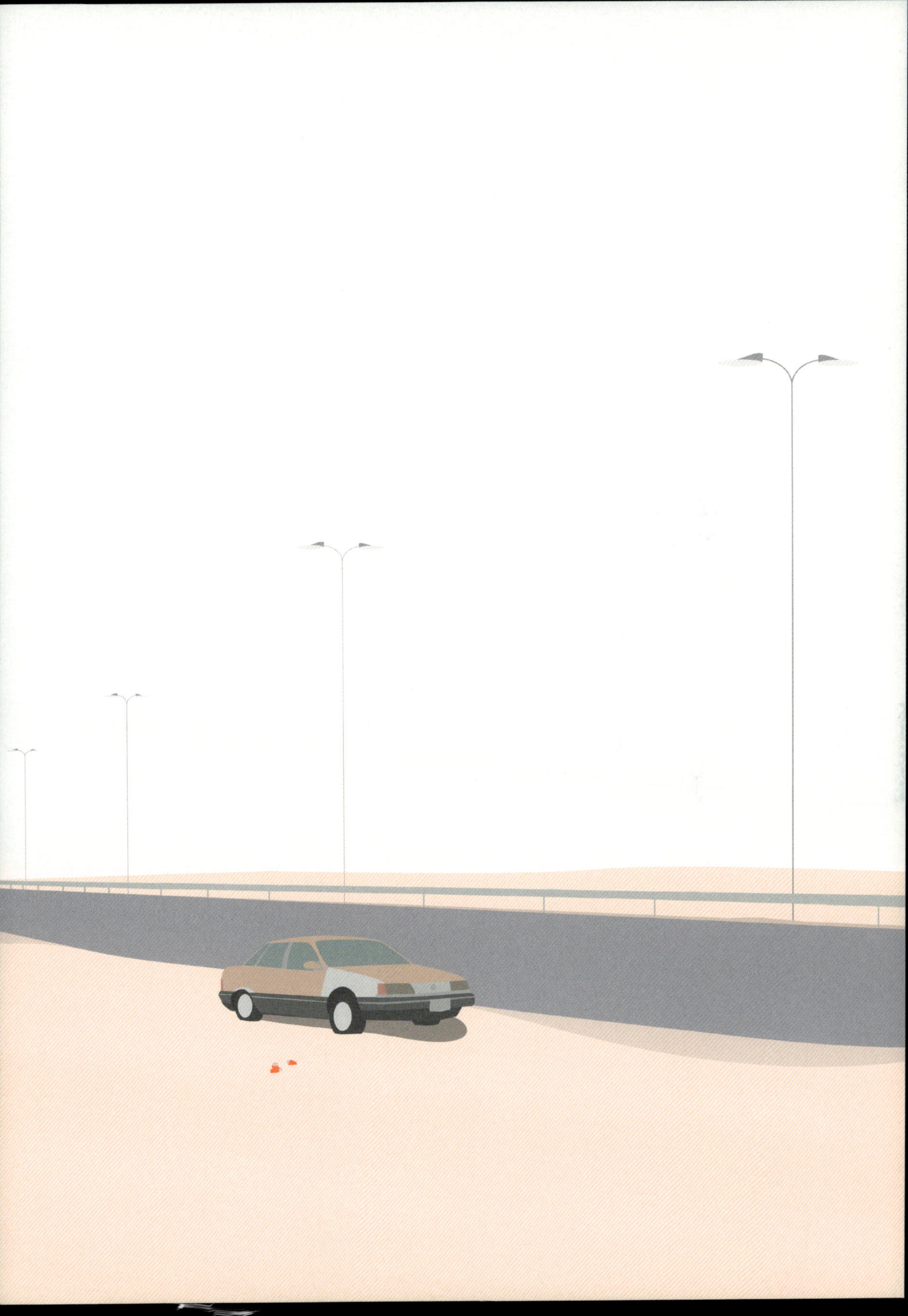

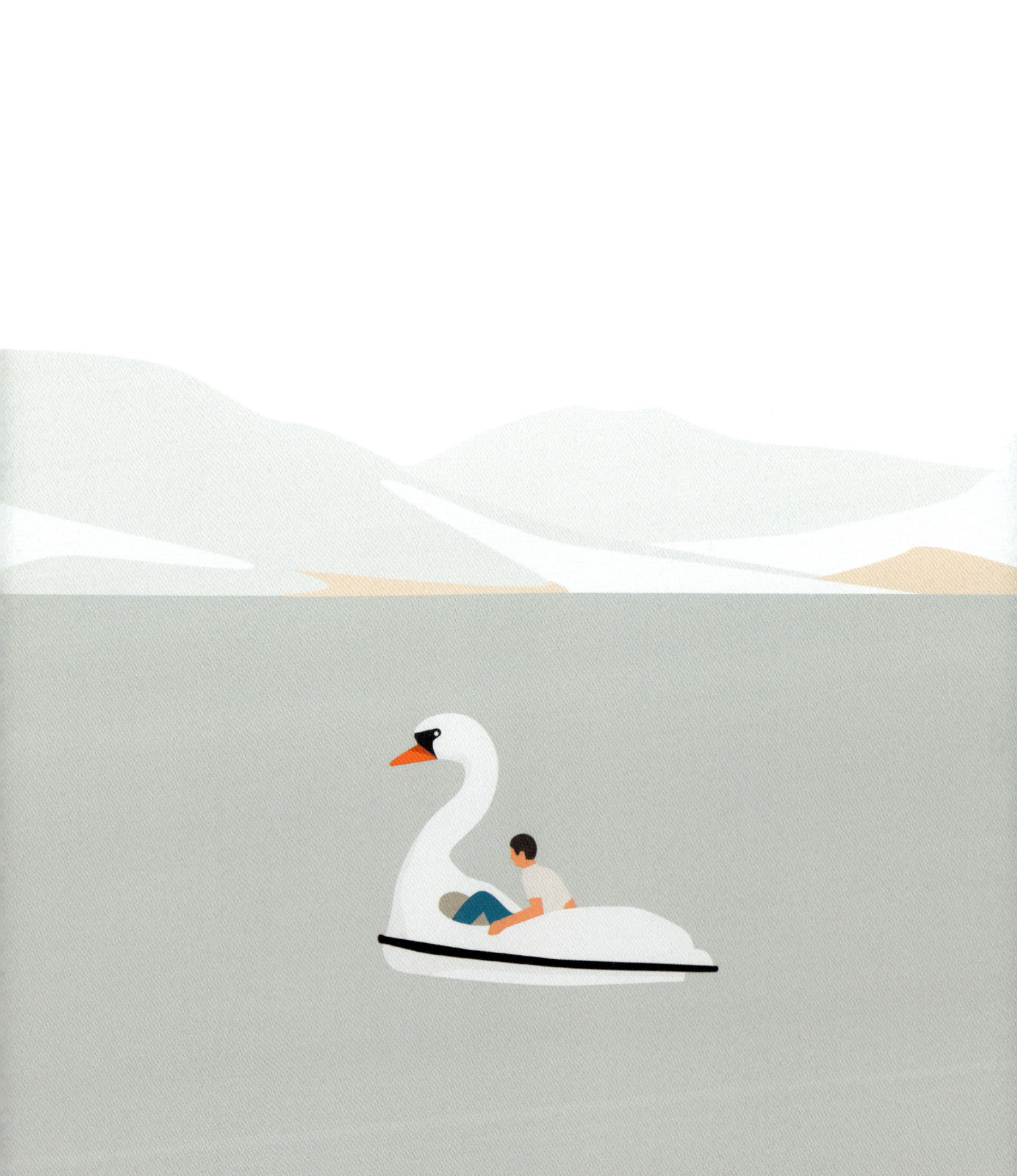

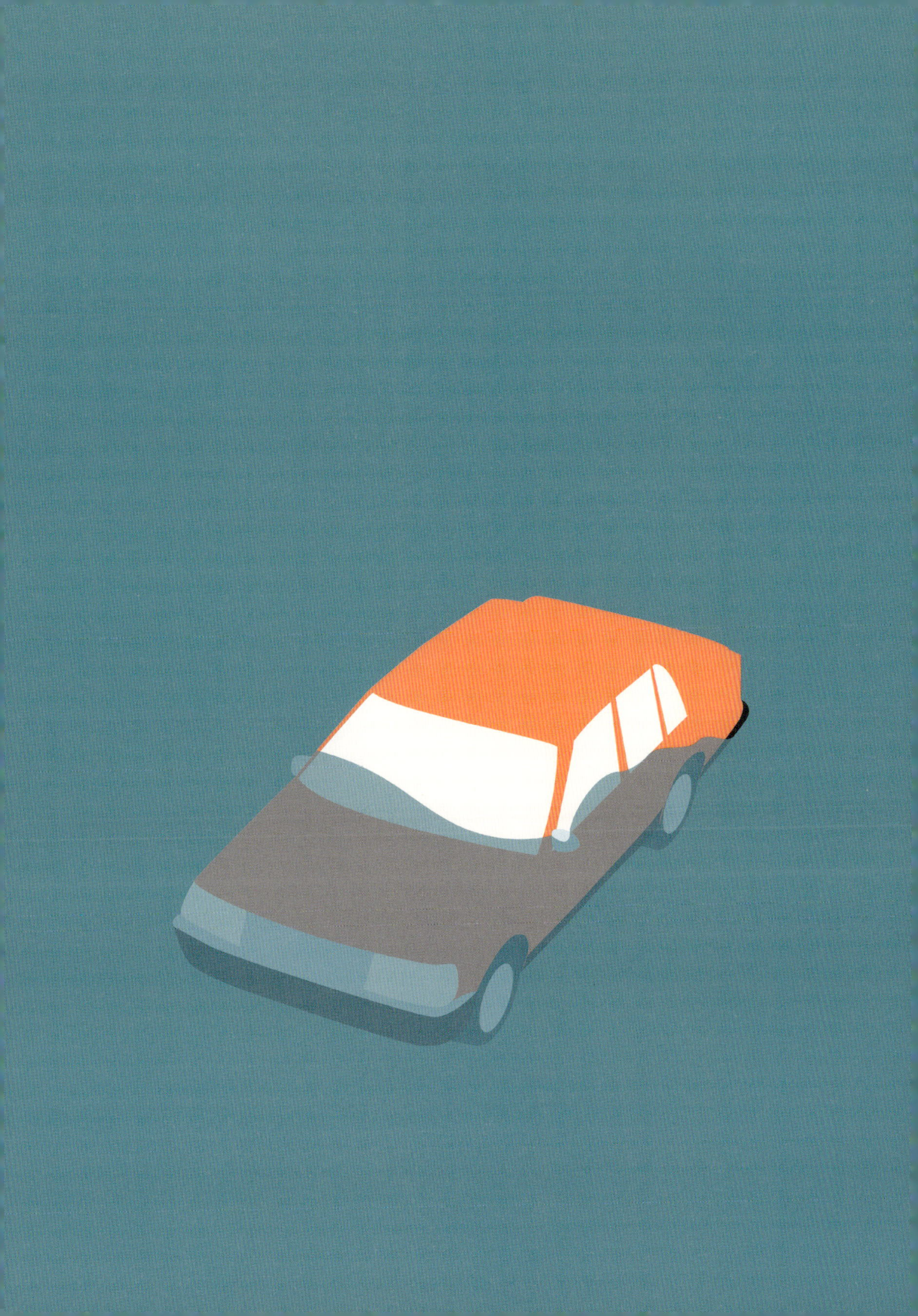

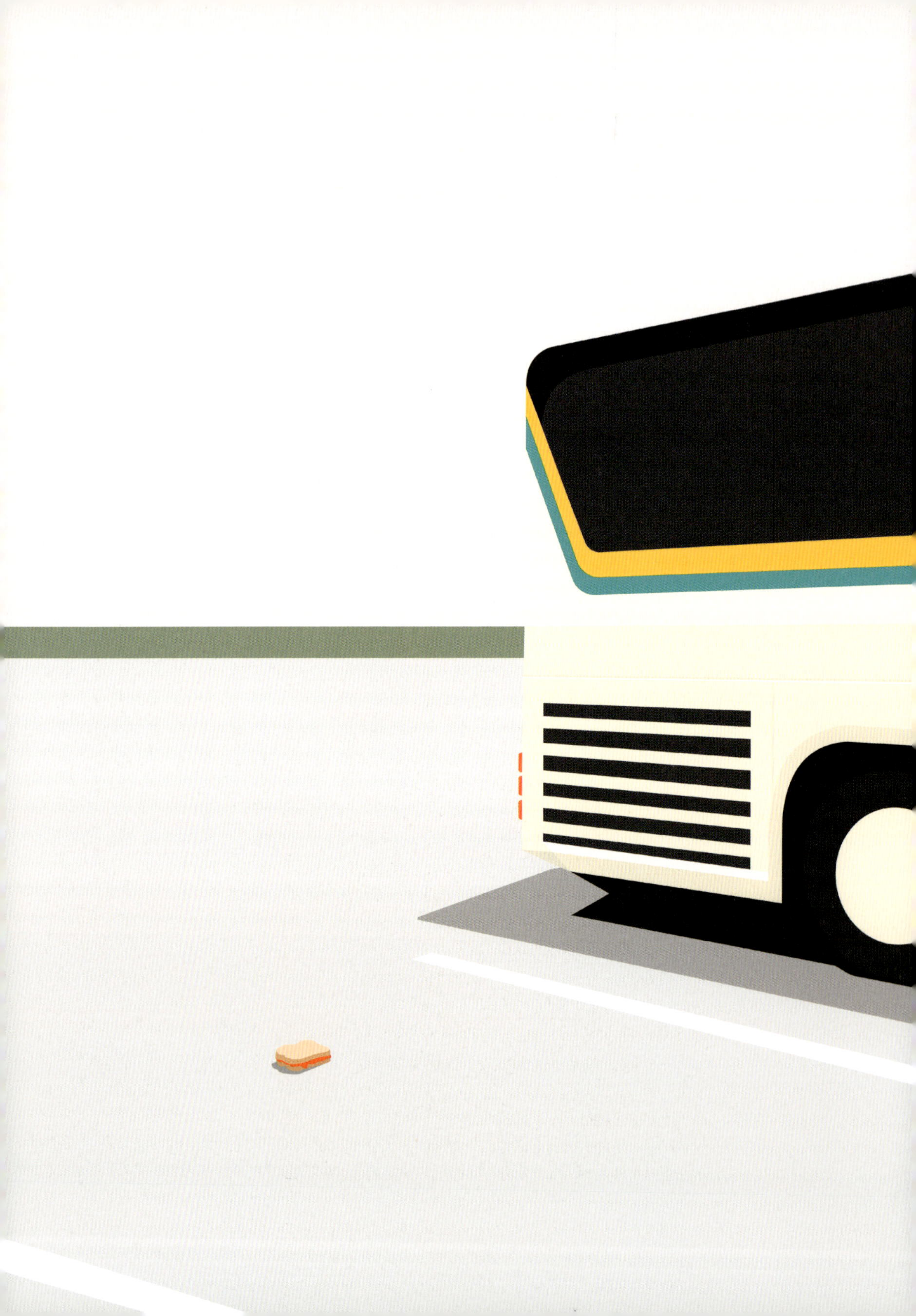

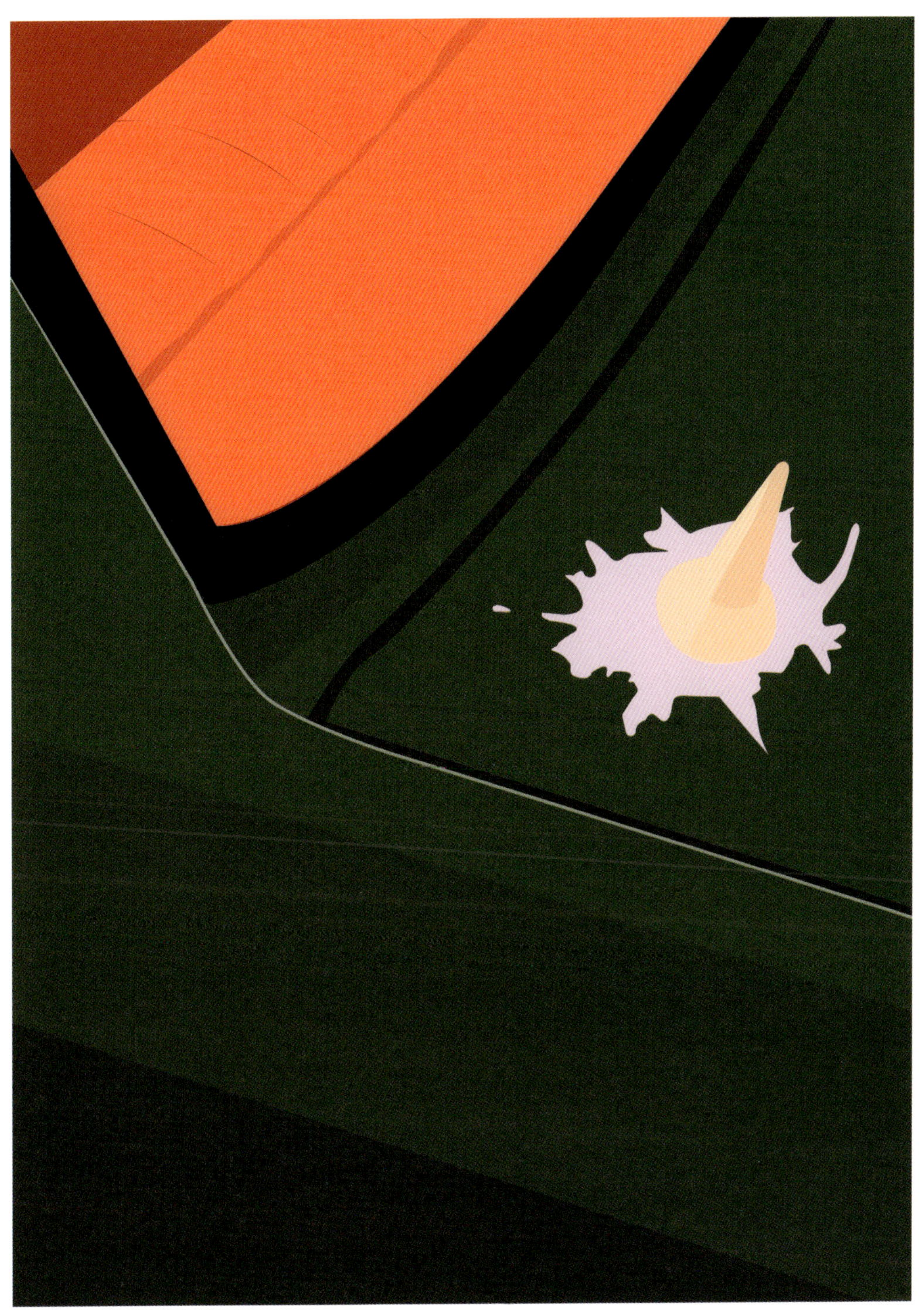

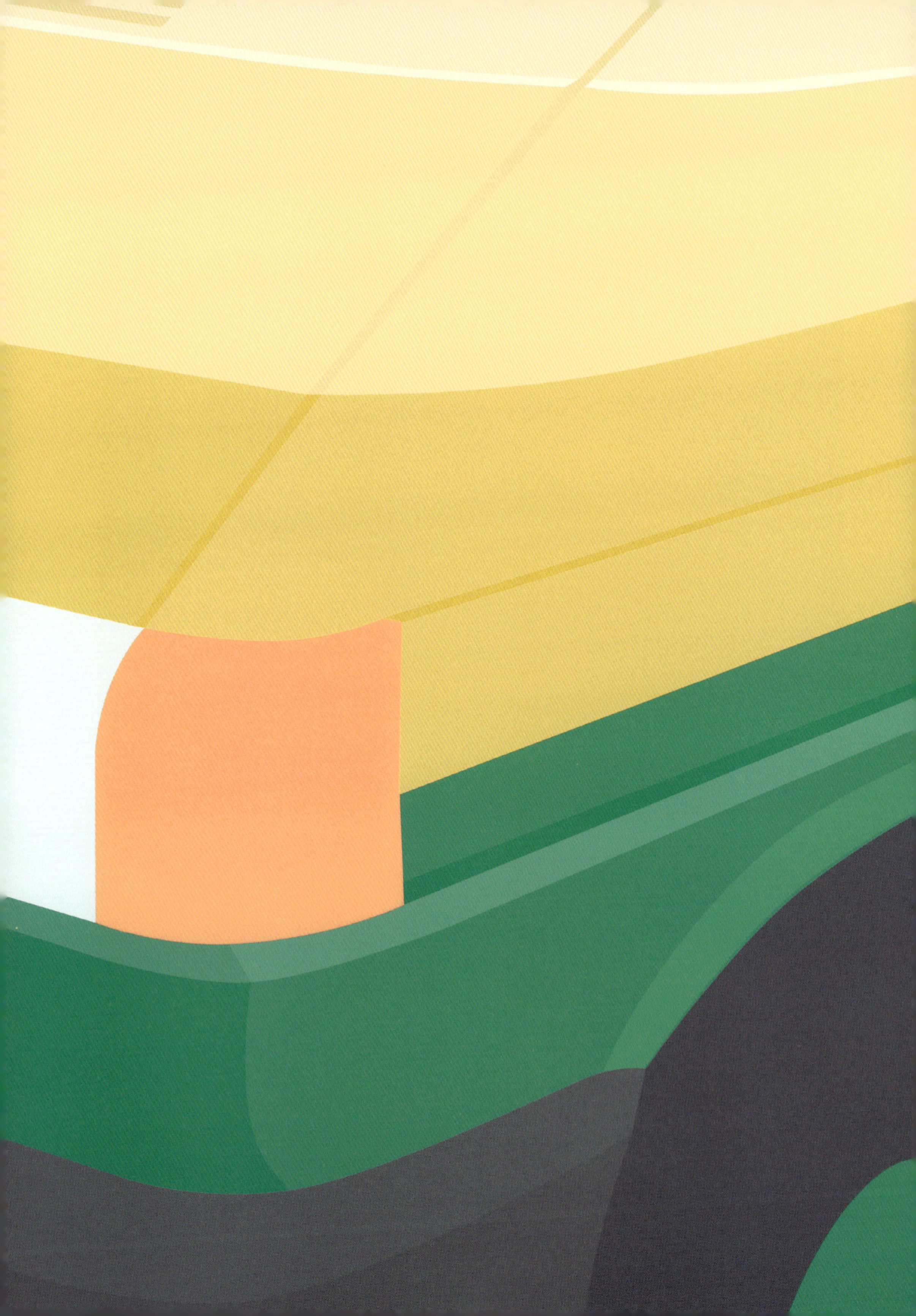

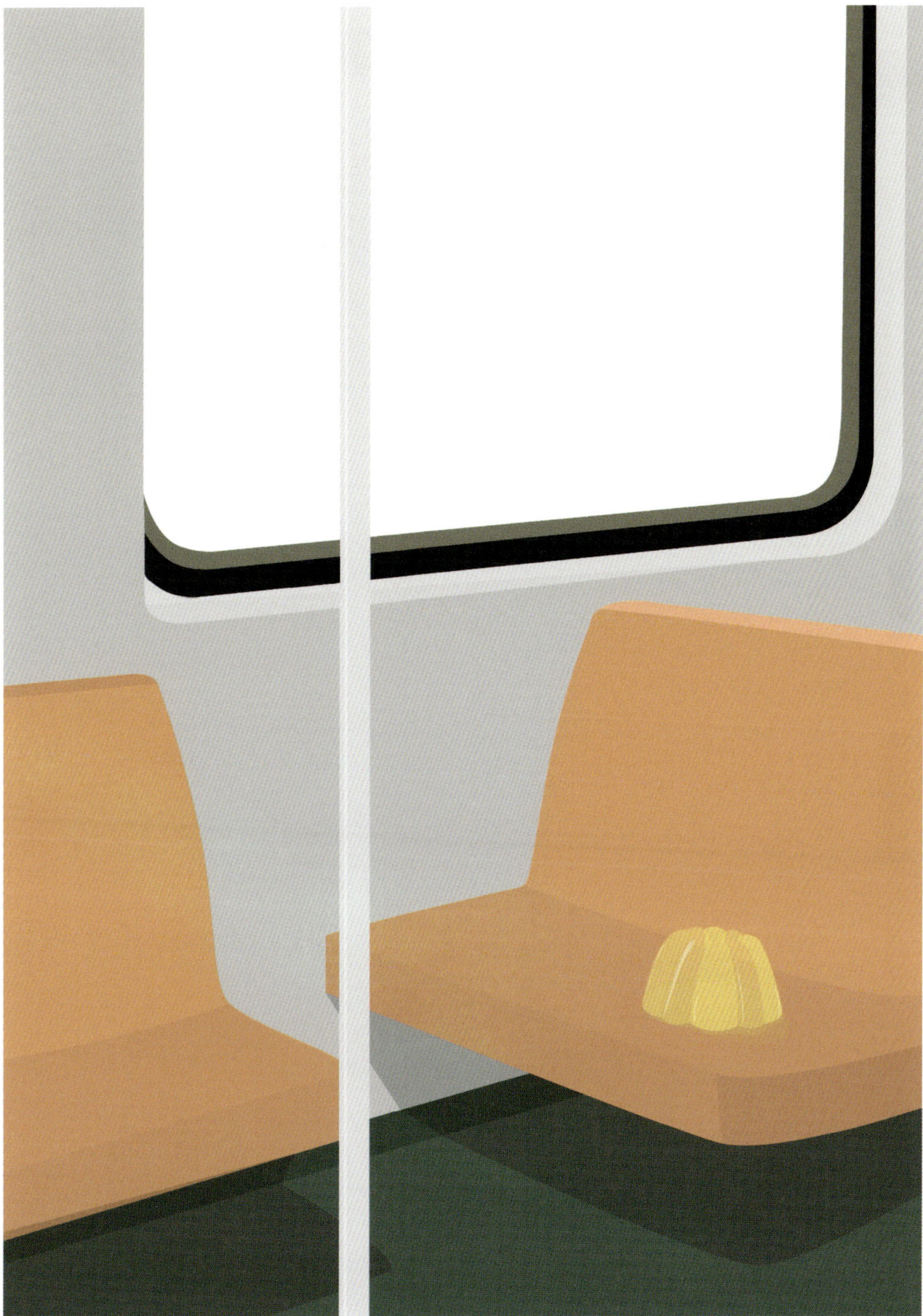

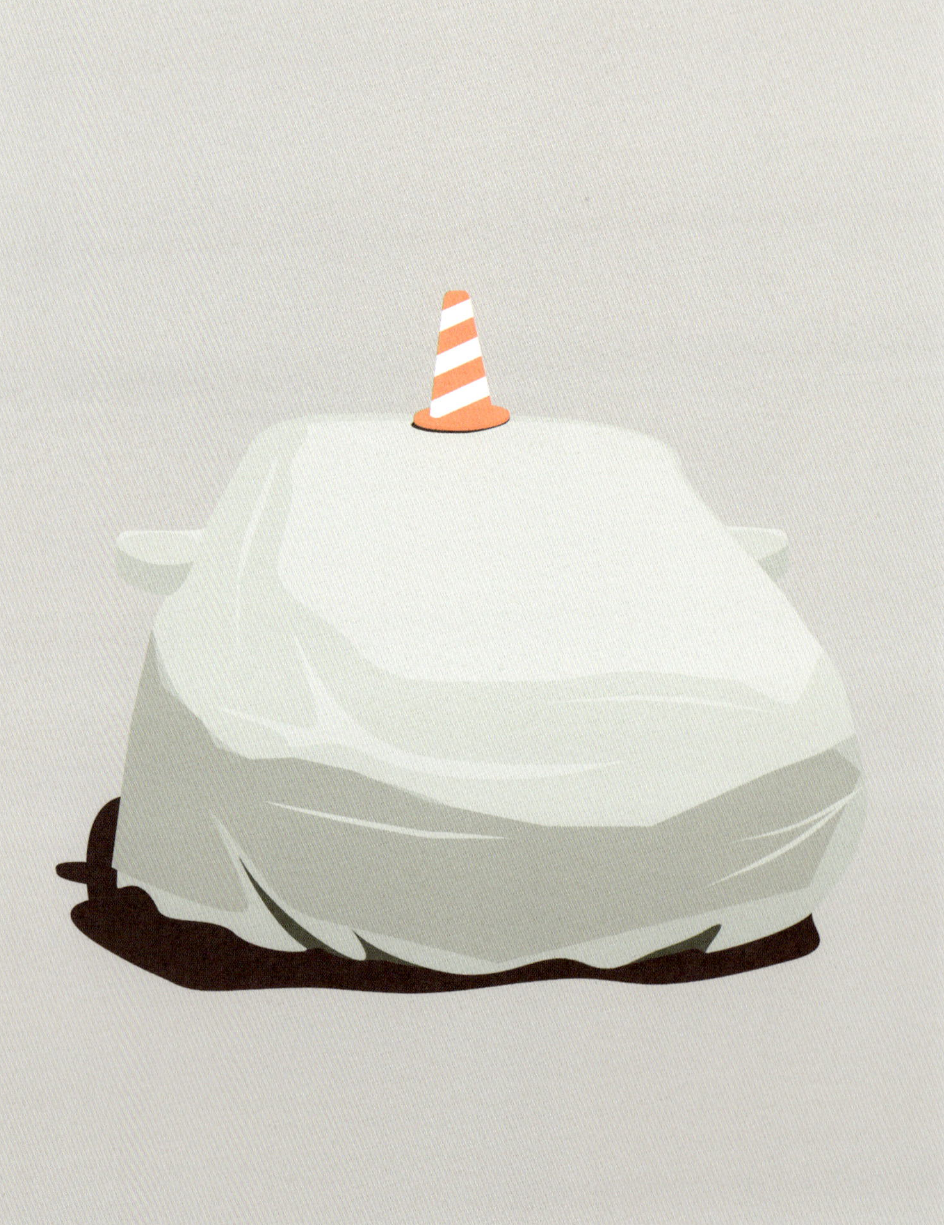

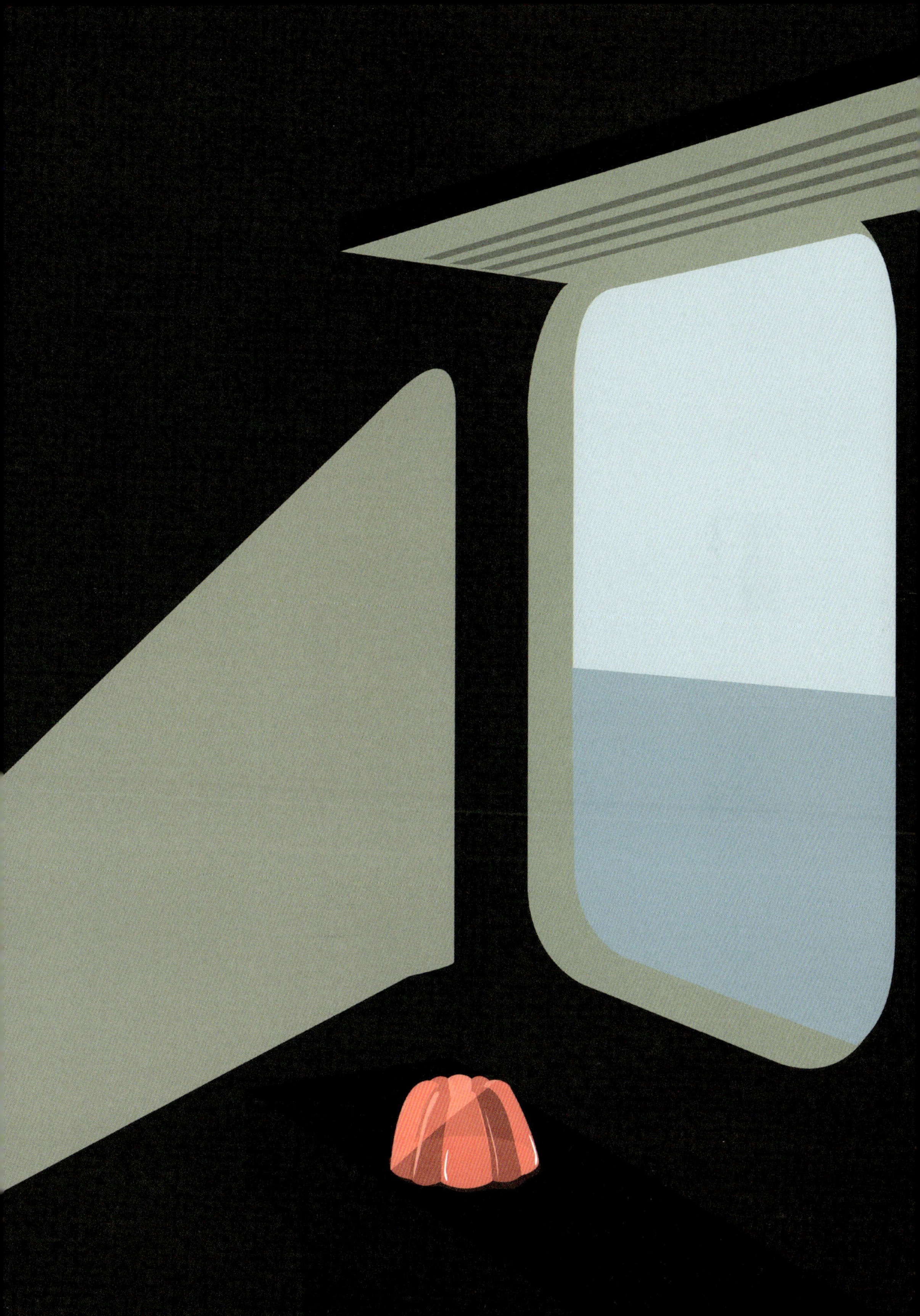

Urban

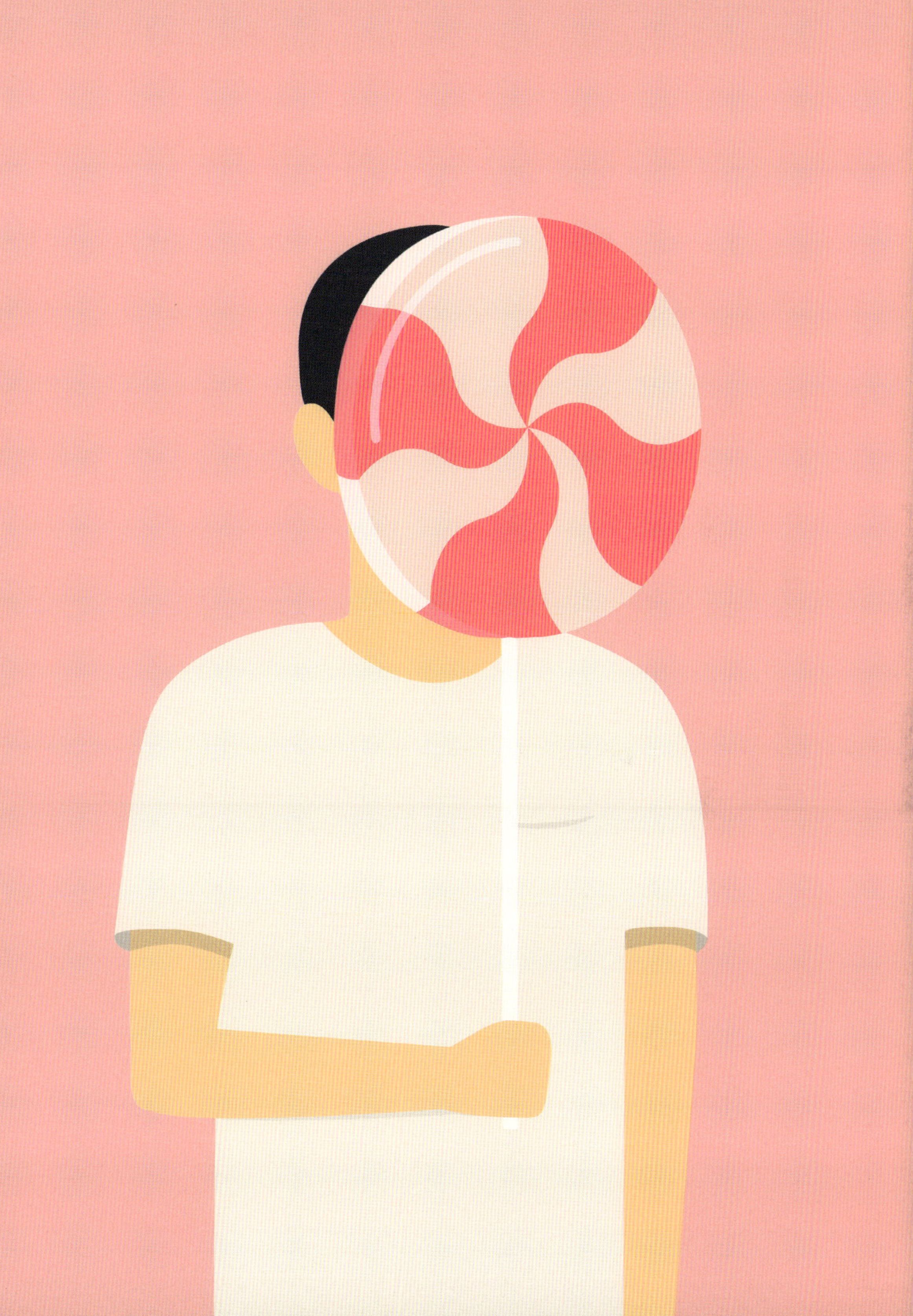

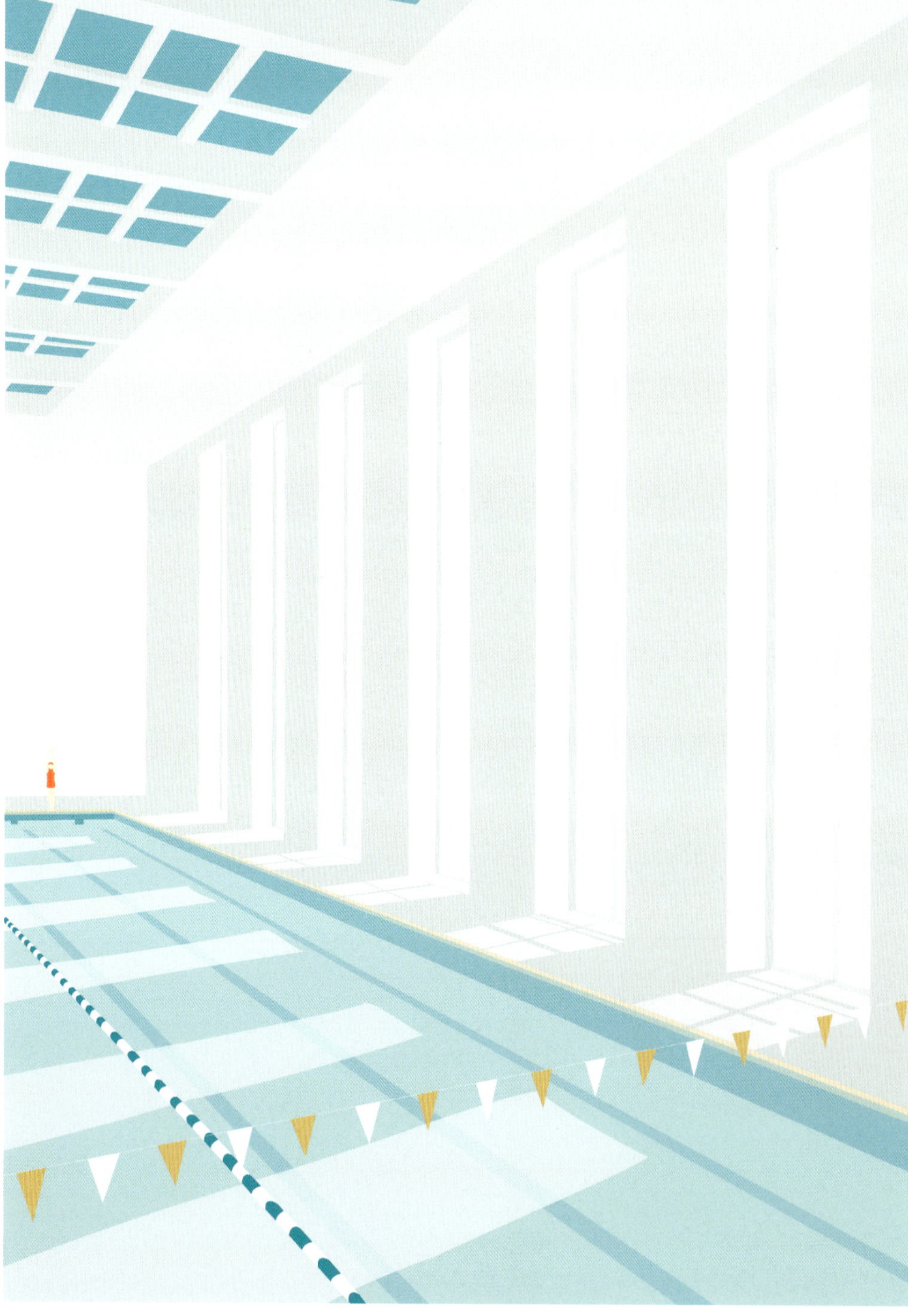

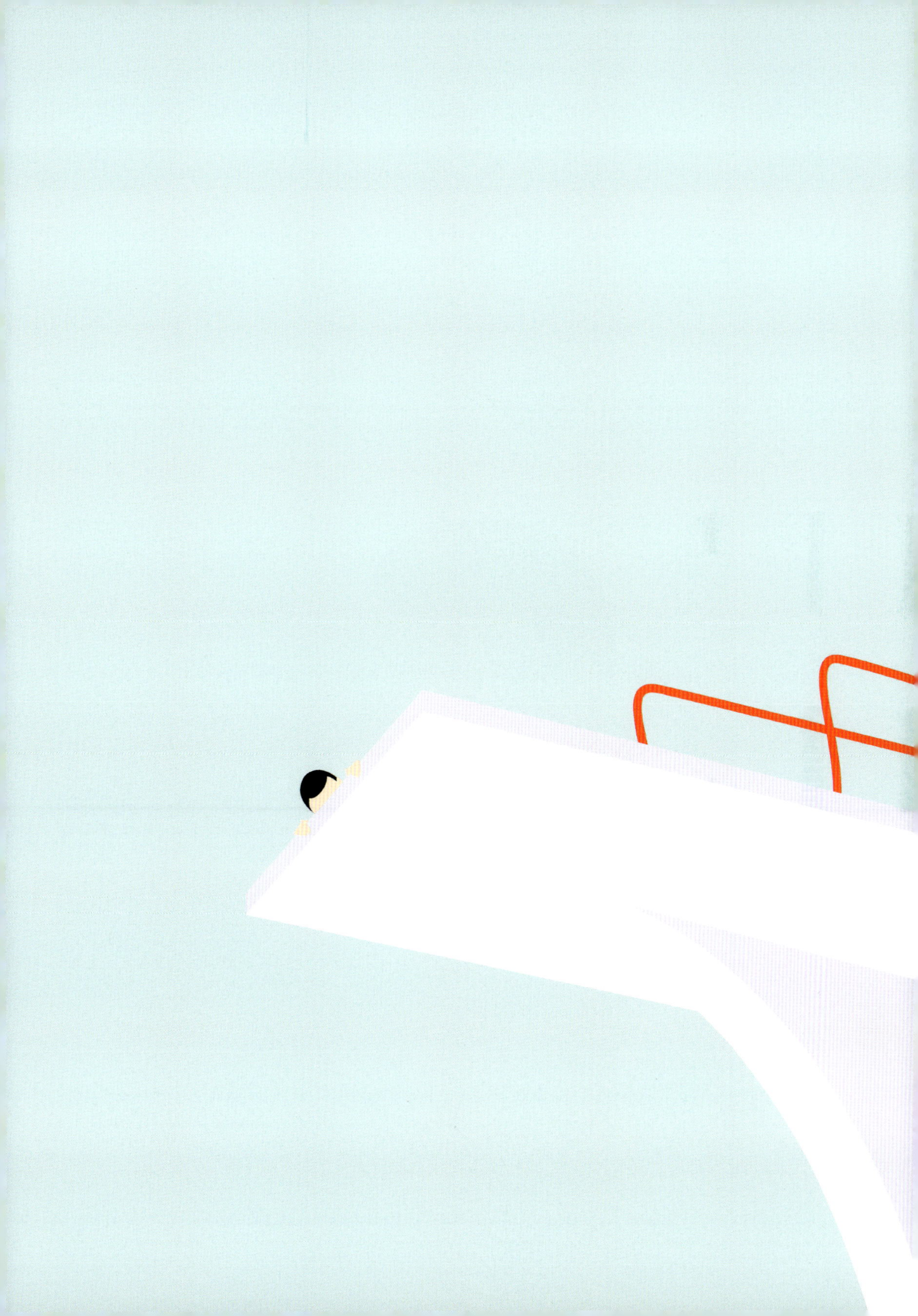

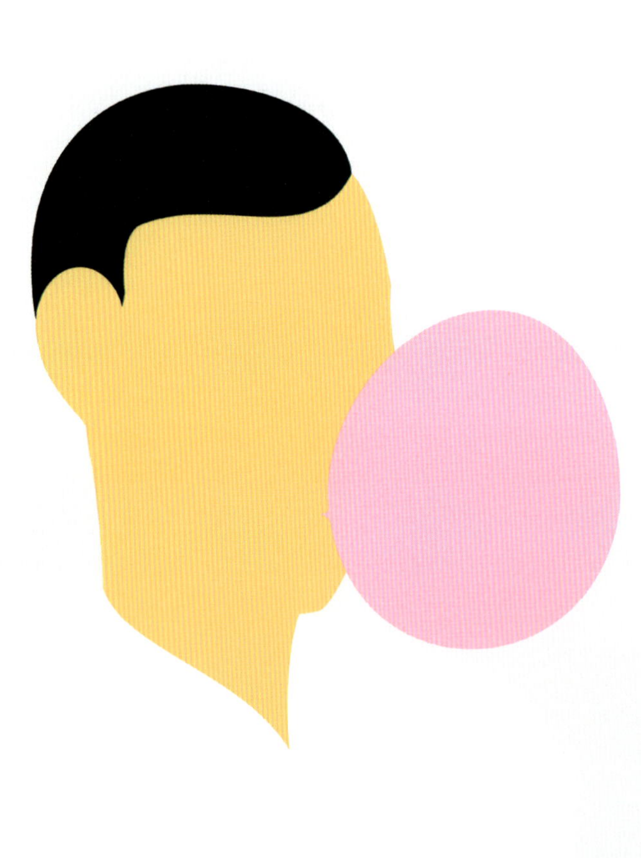

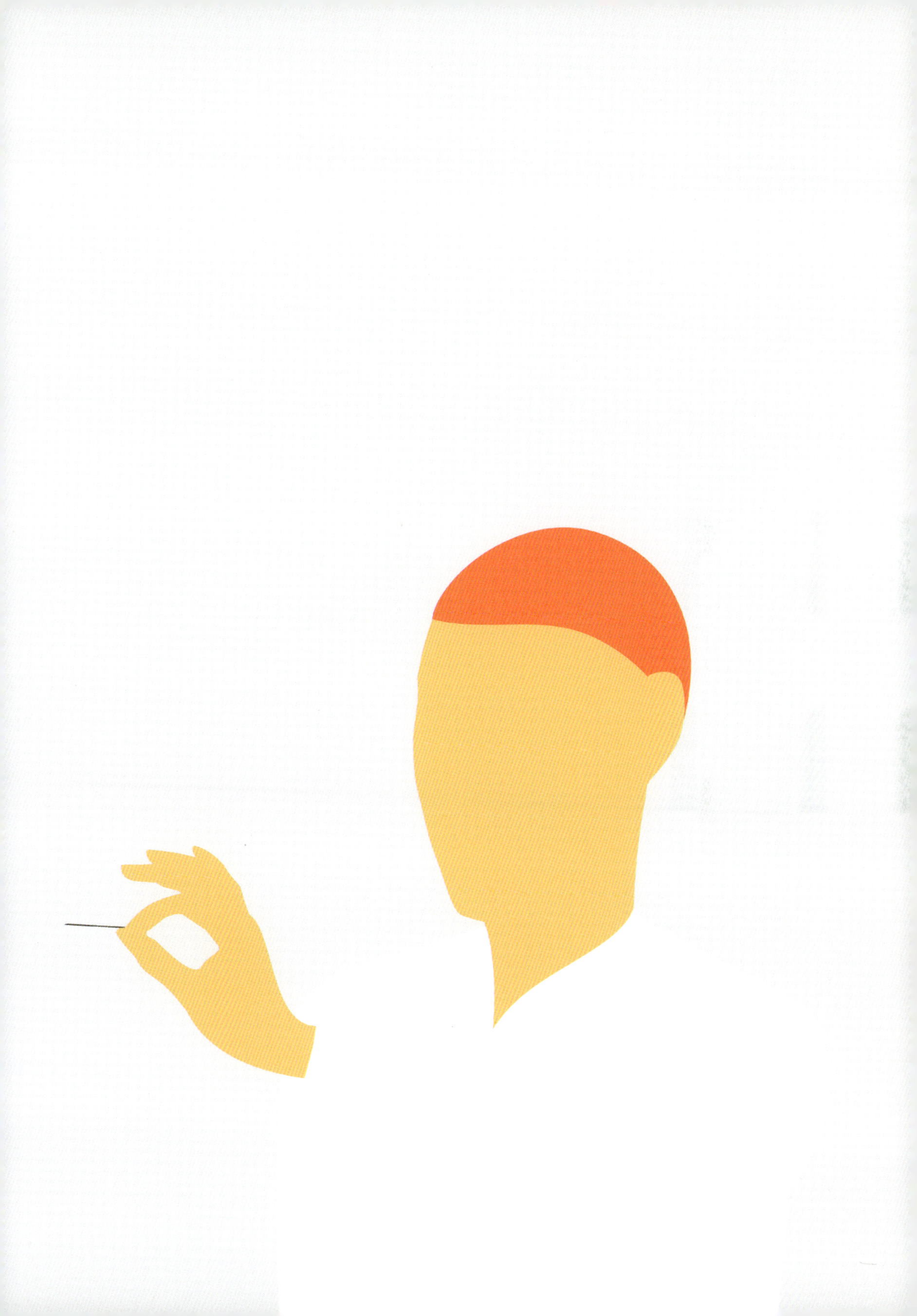

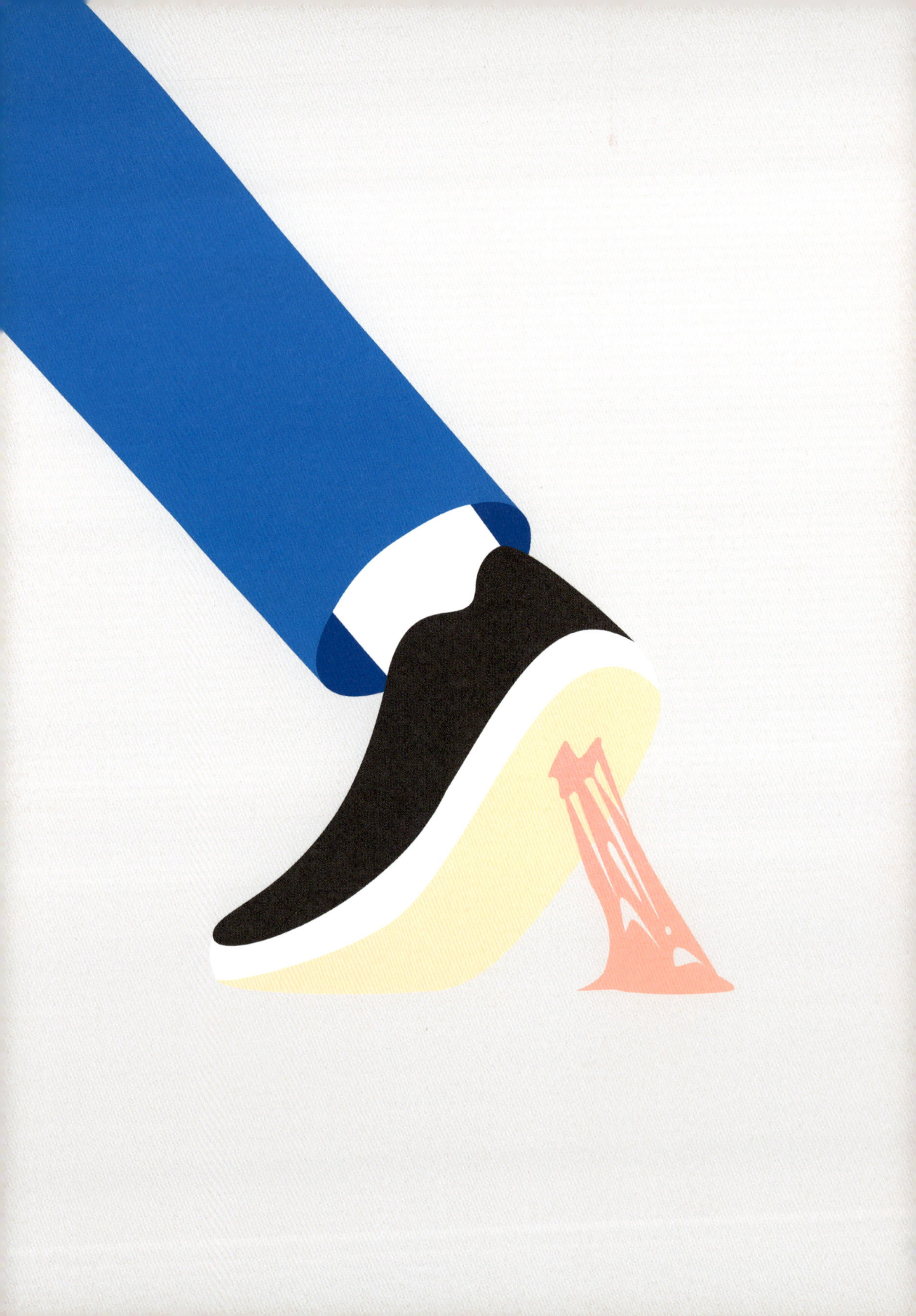

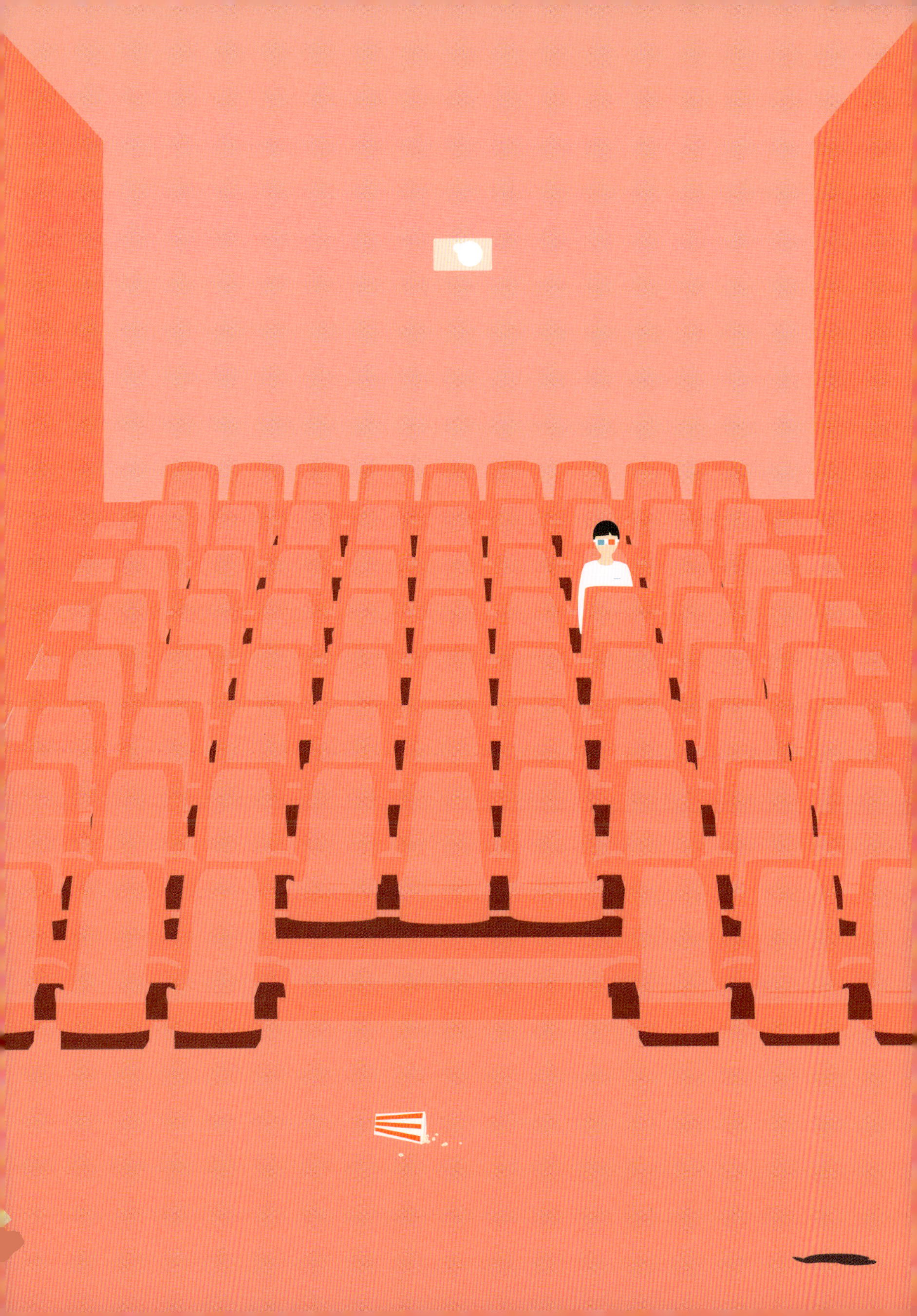

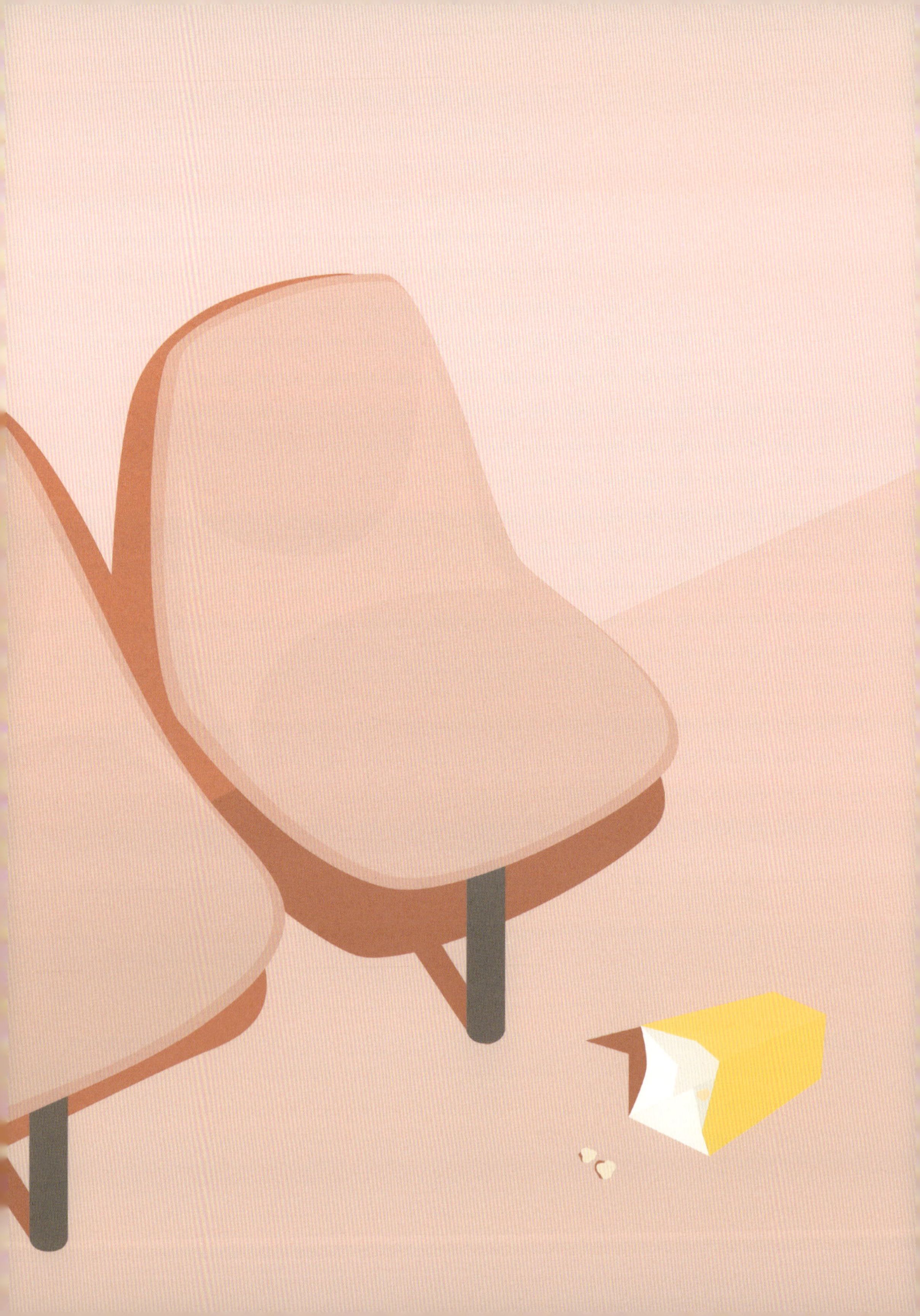

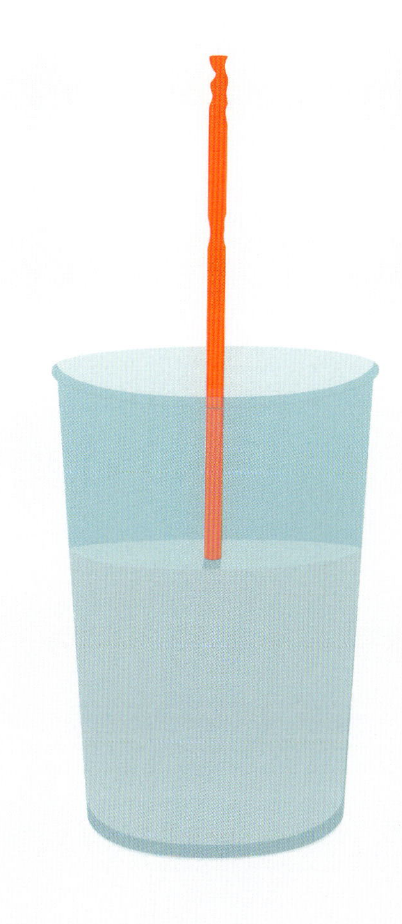

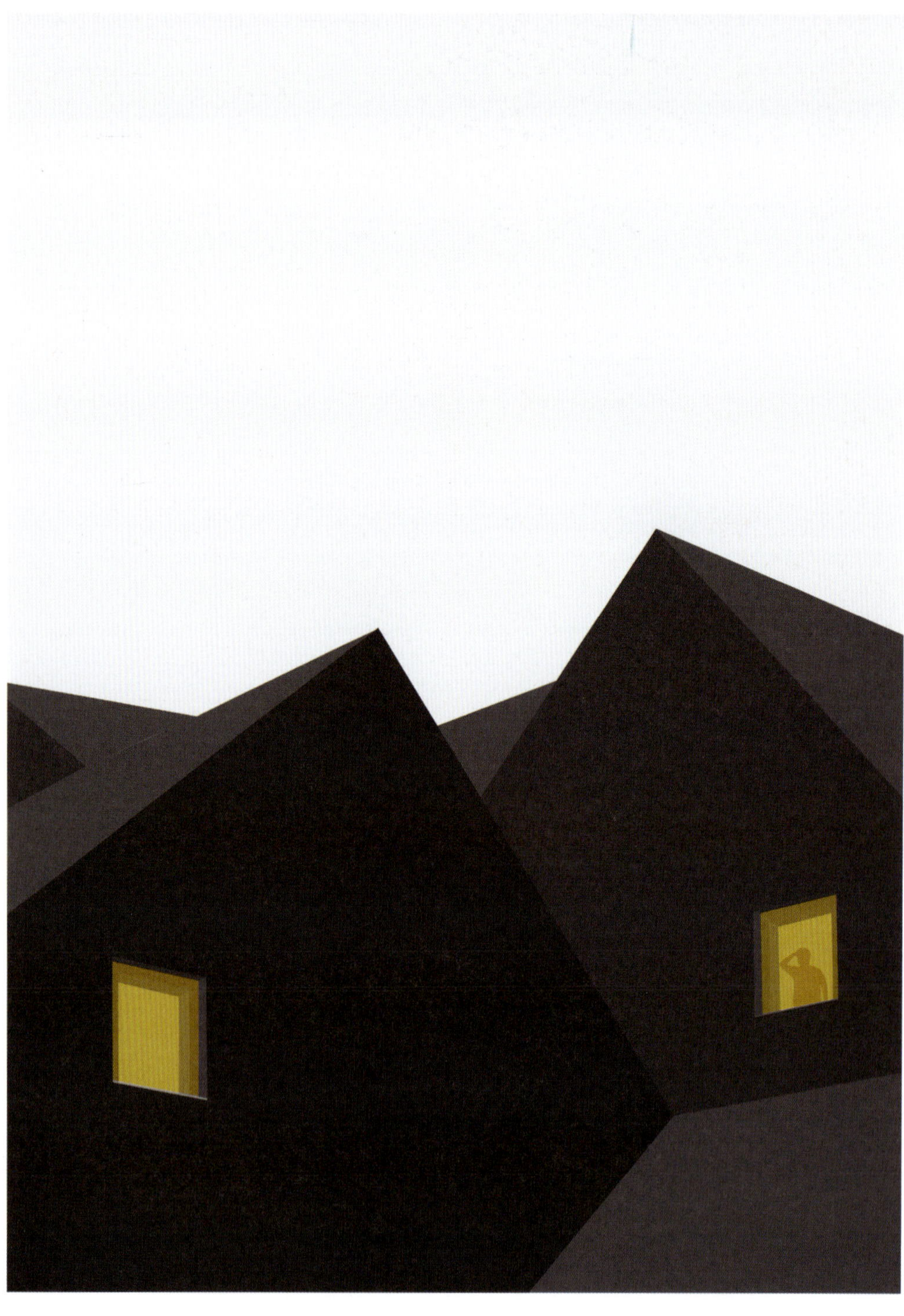

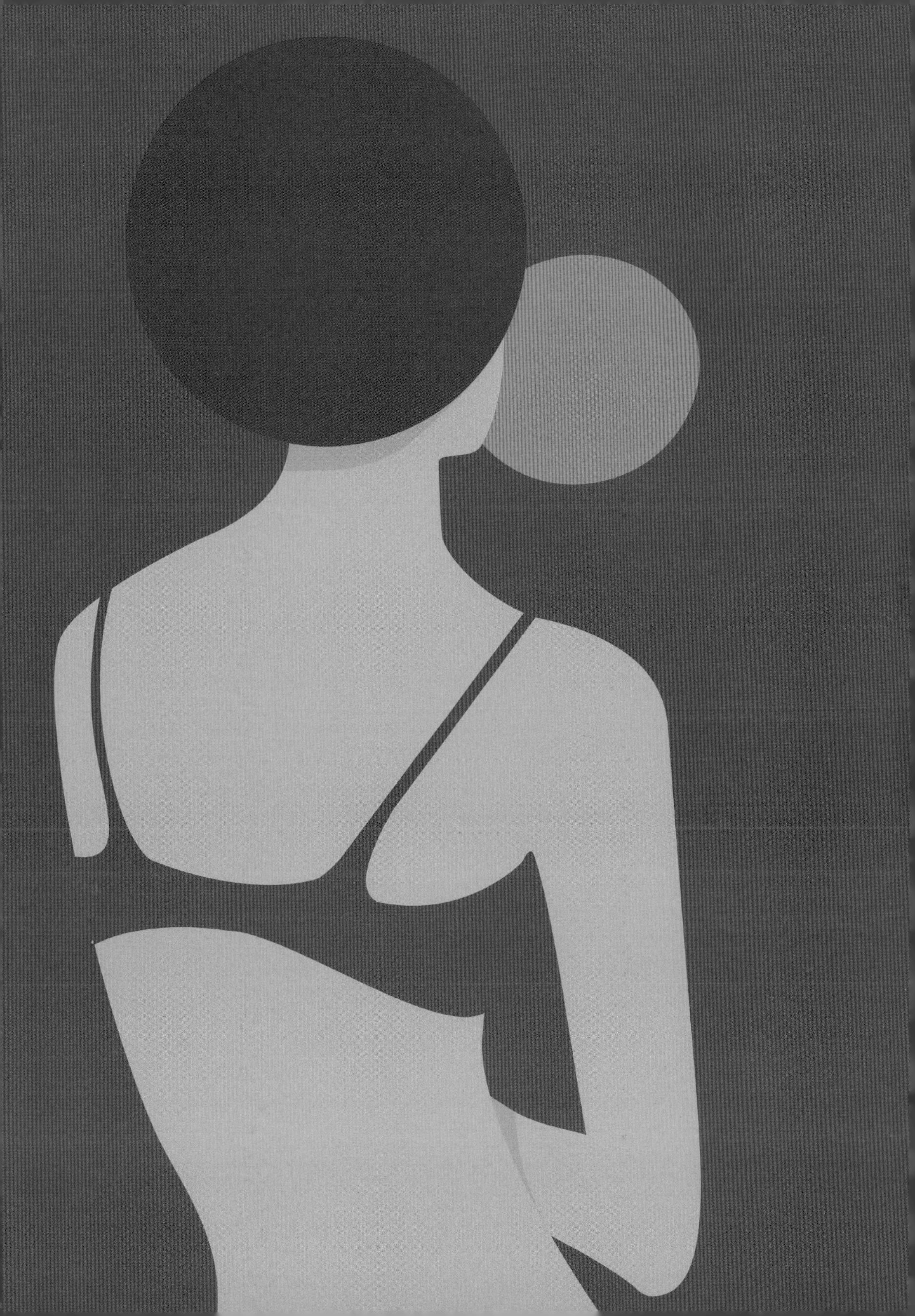

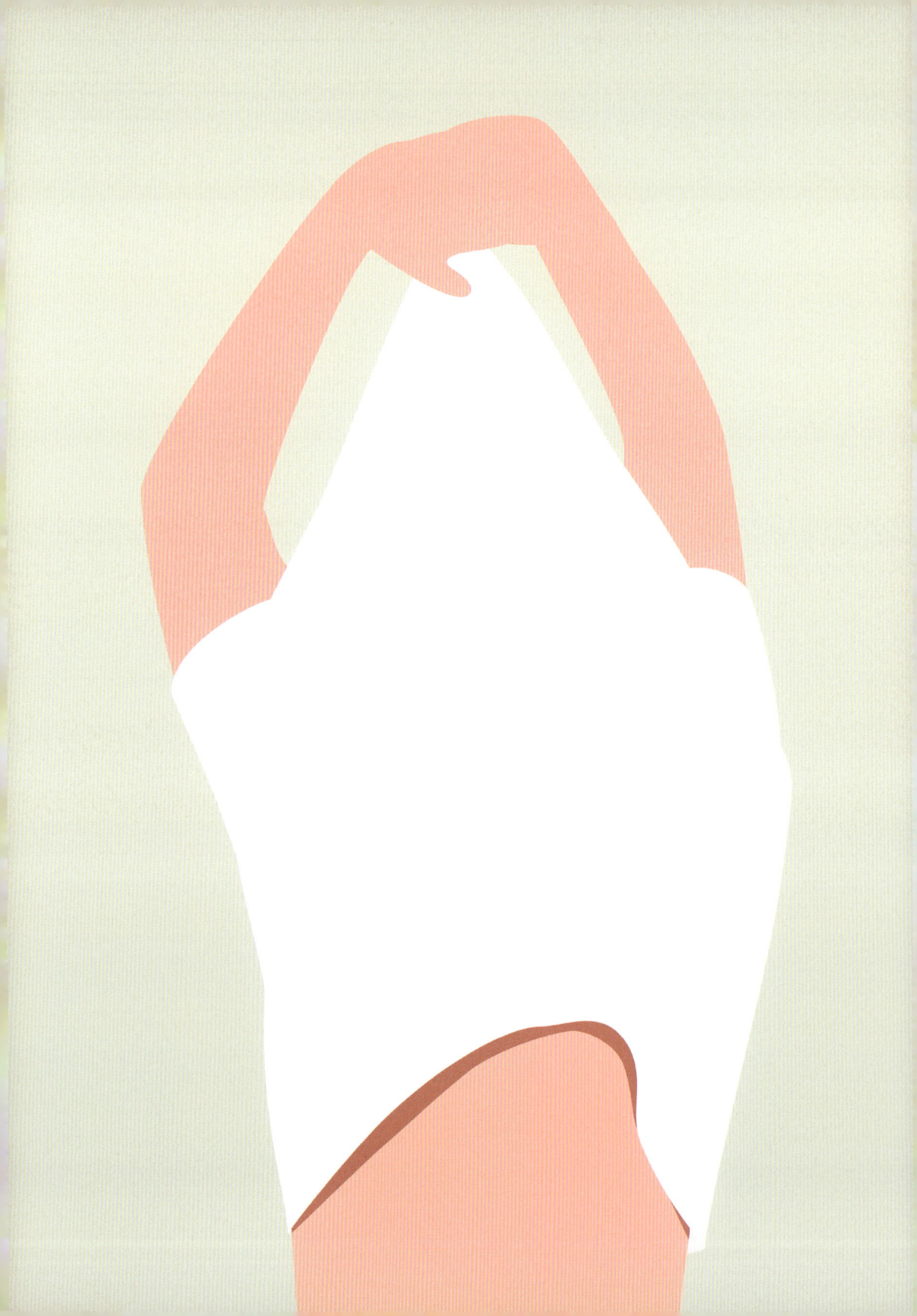

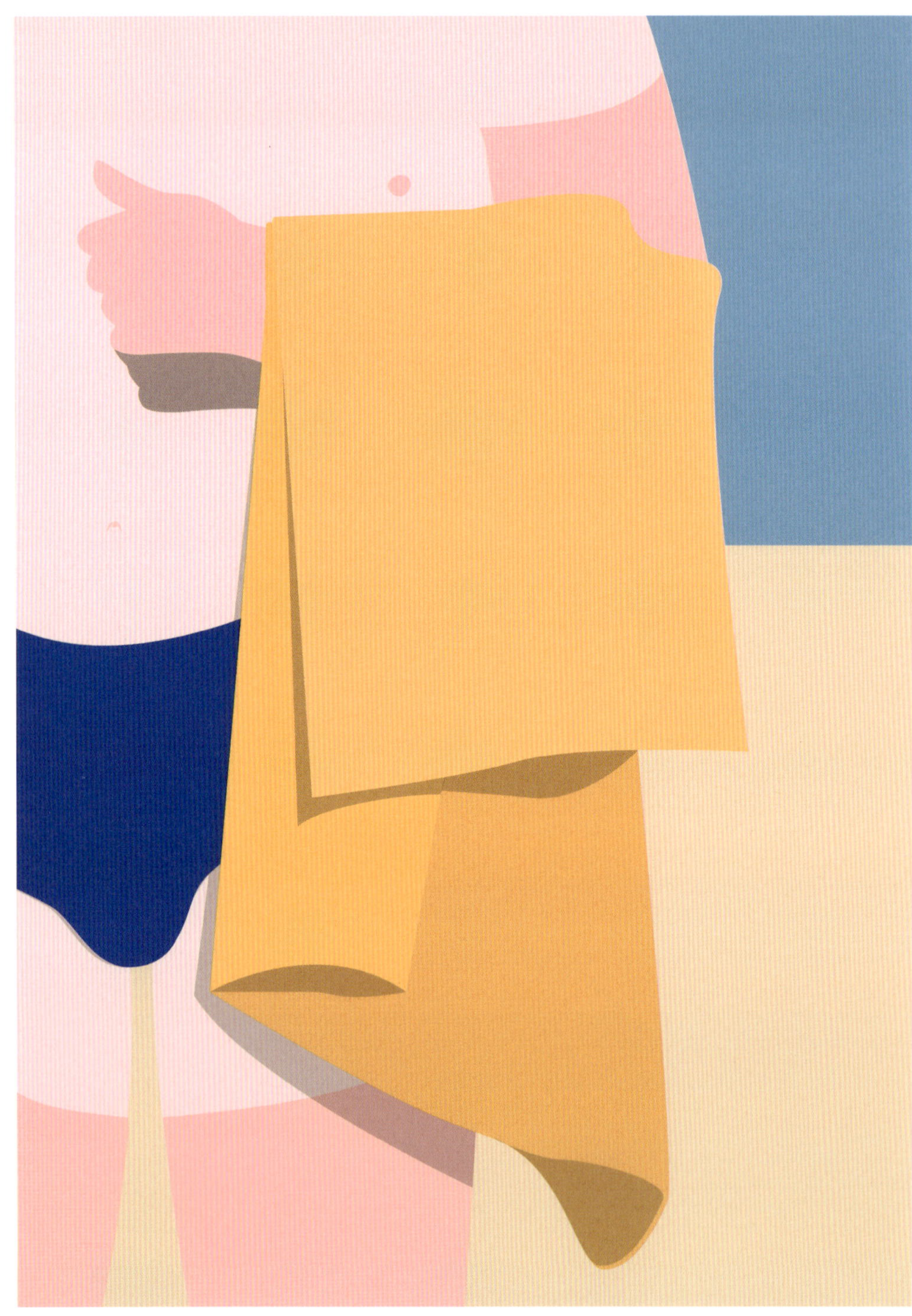

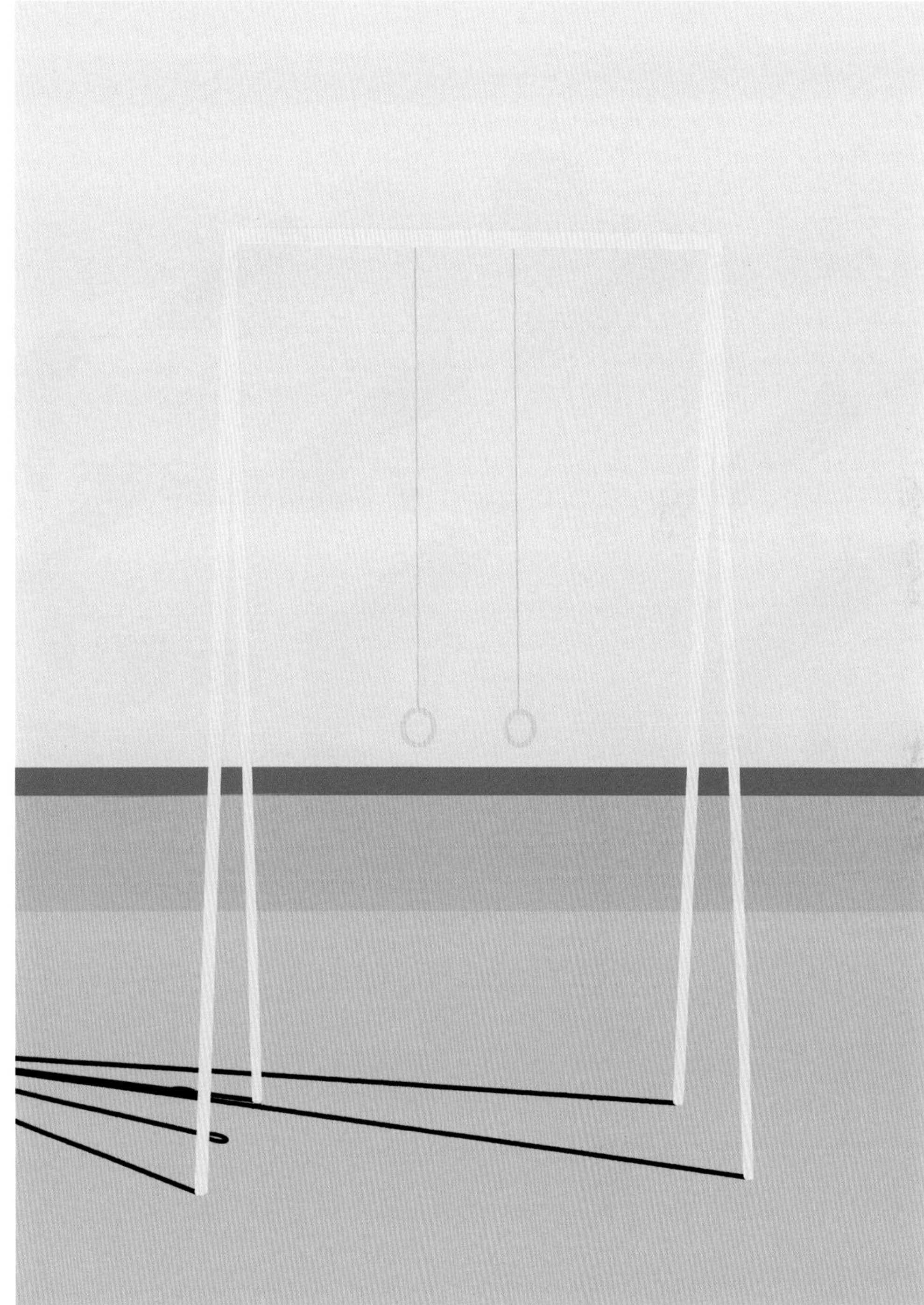

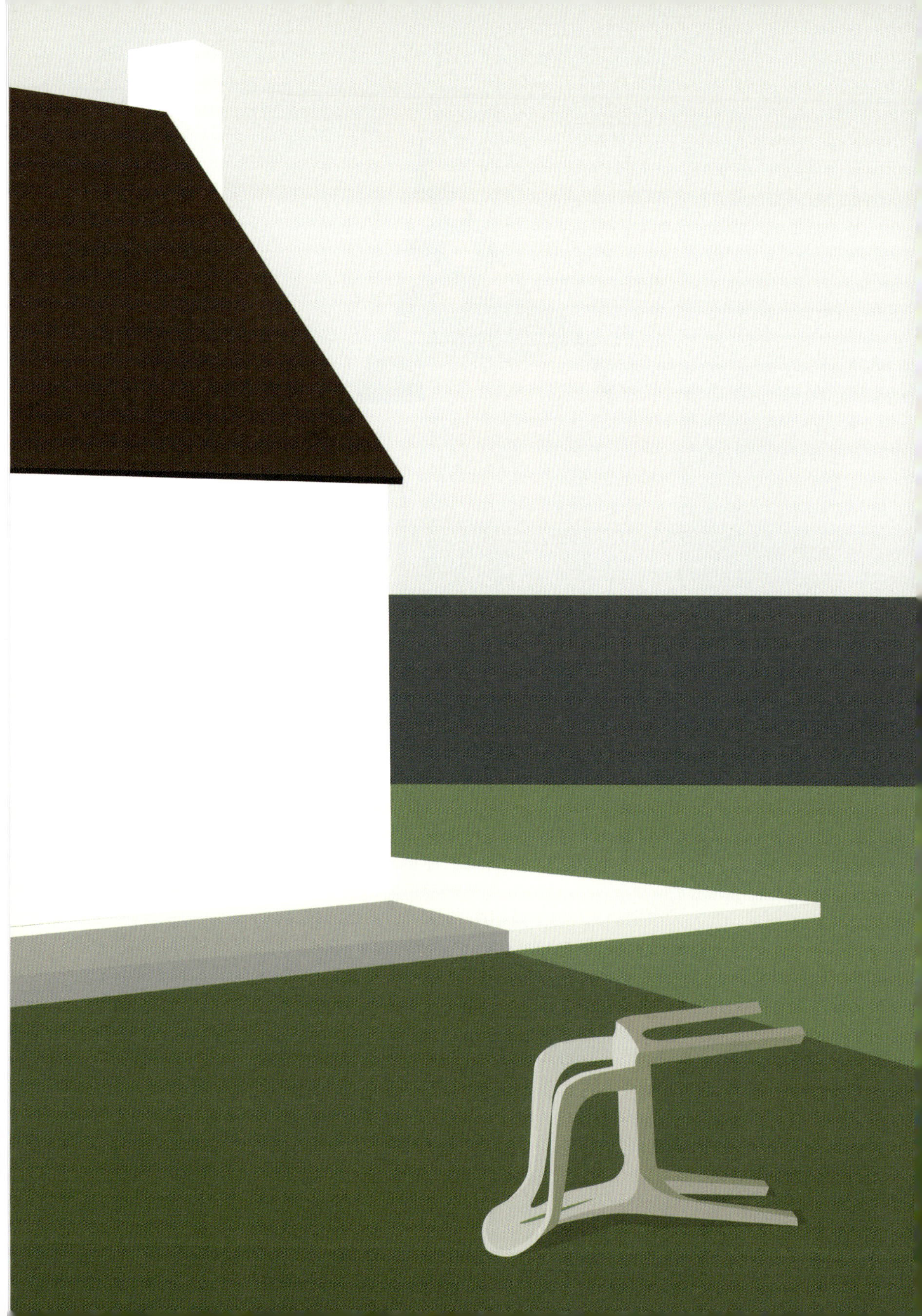

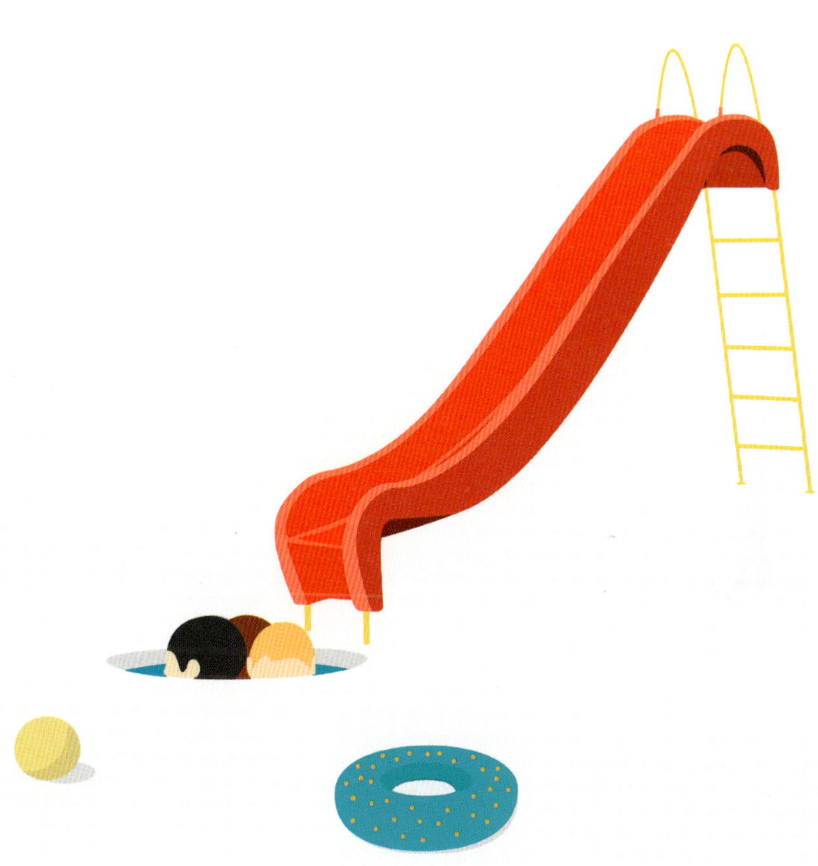

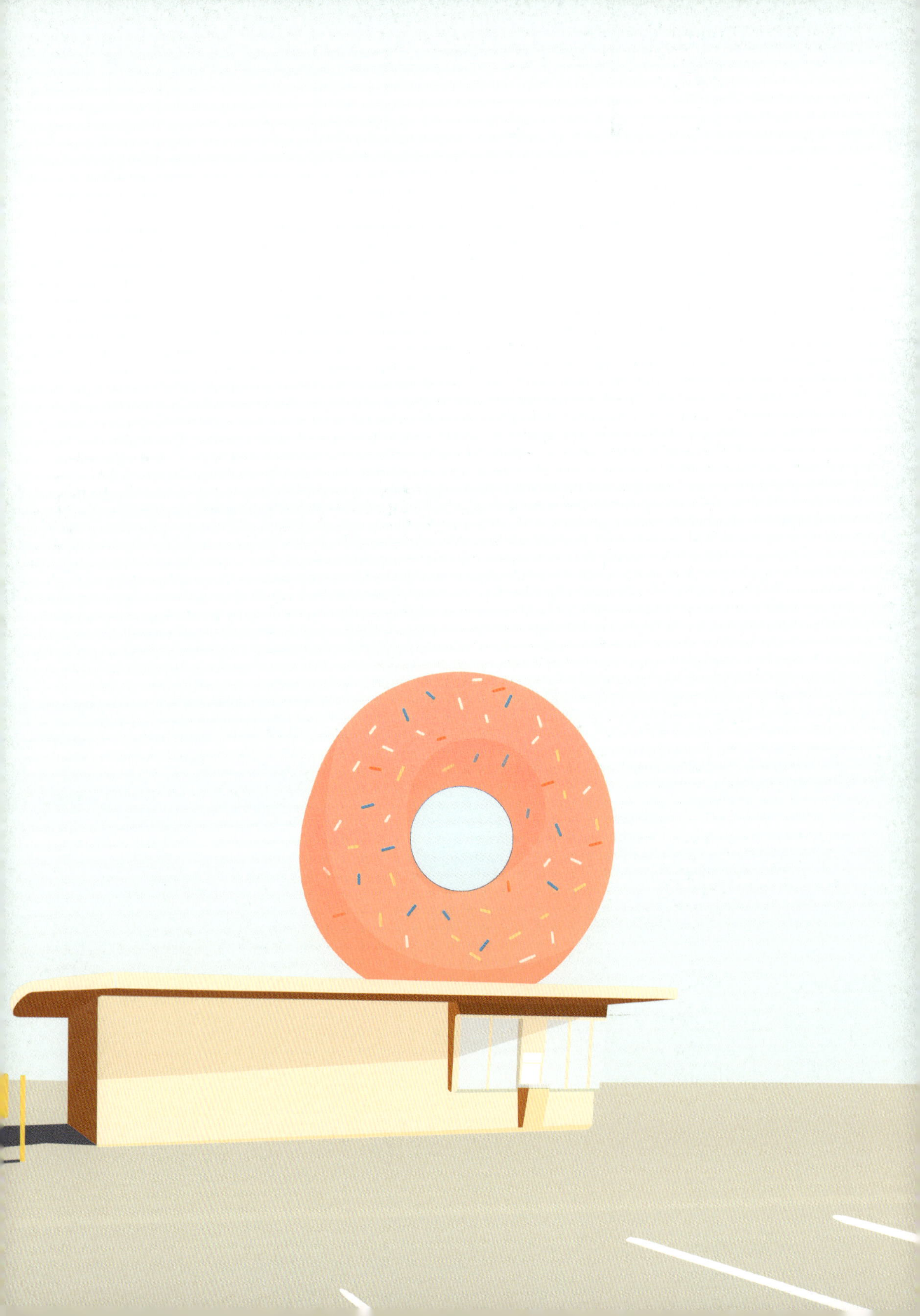

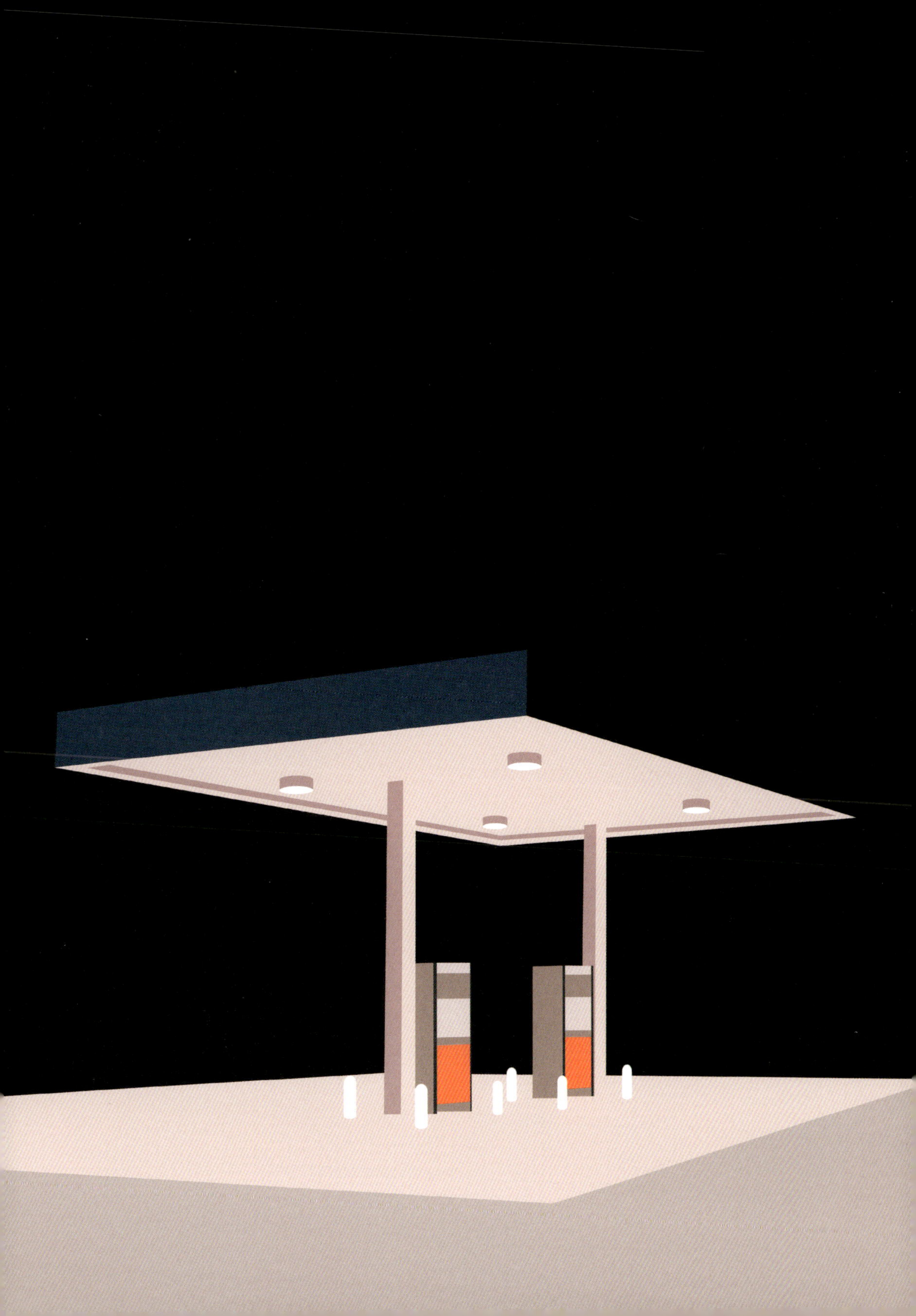

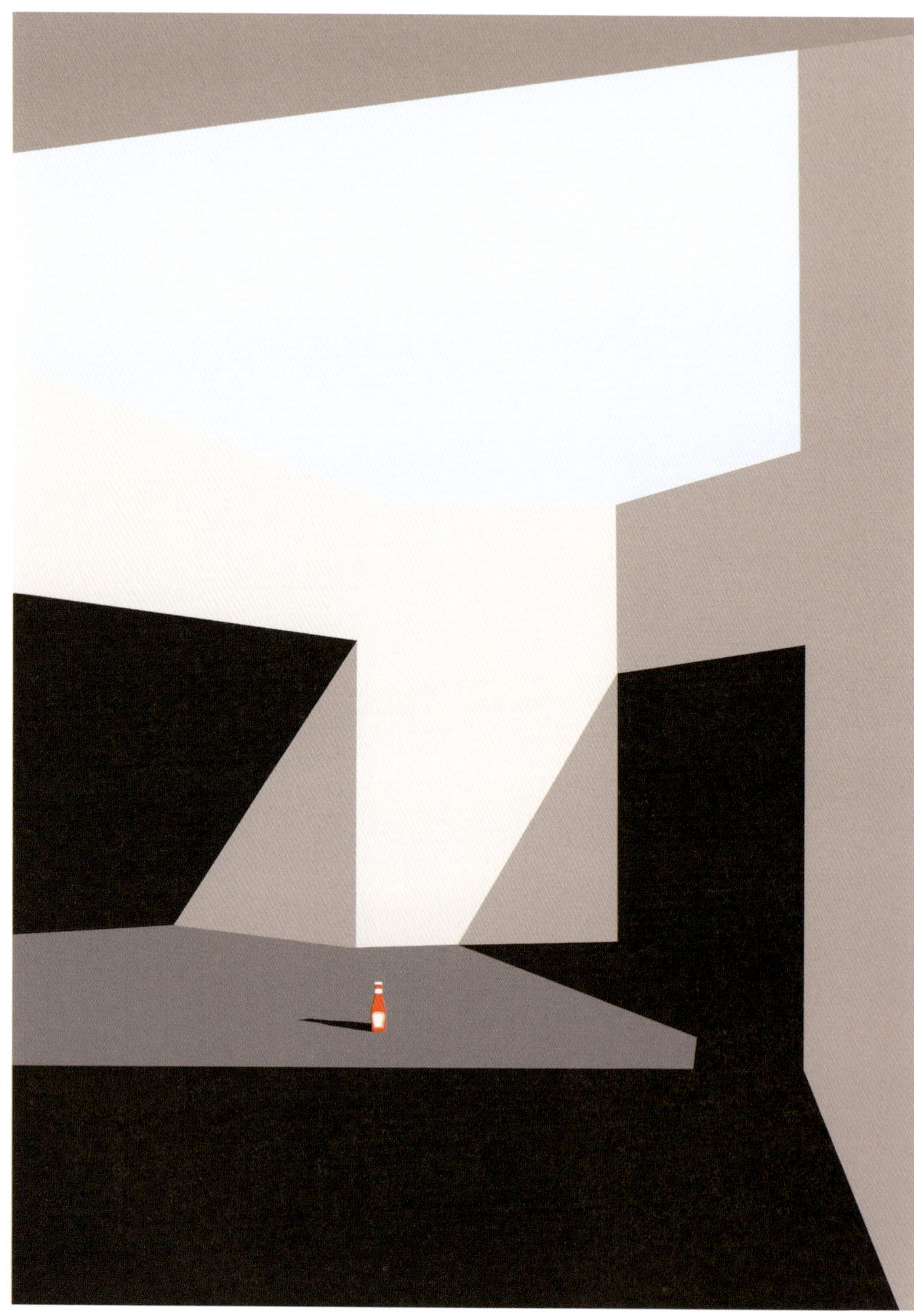

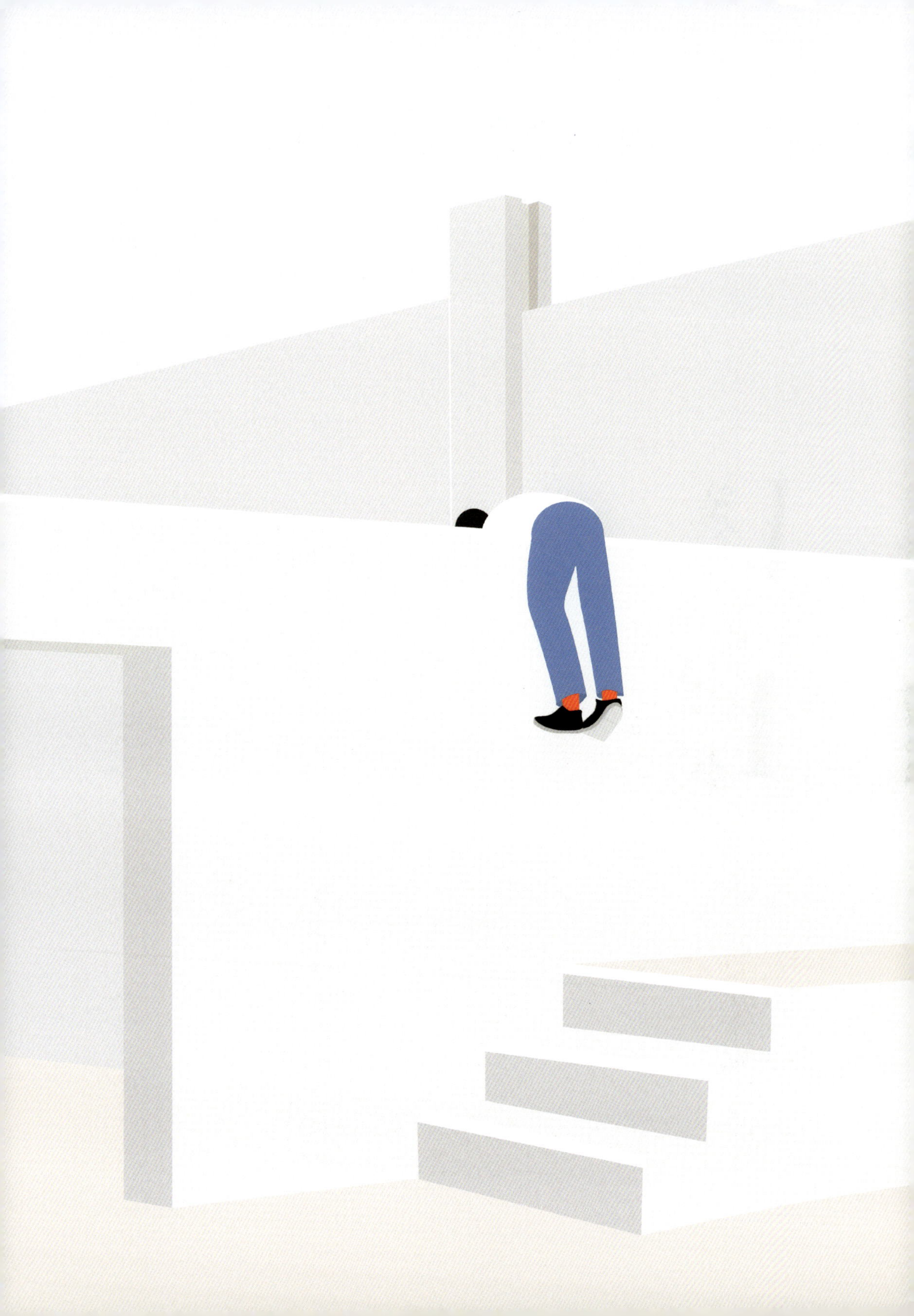

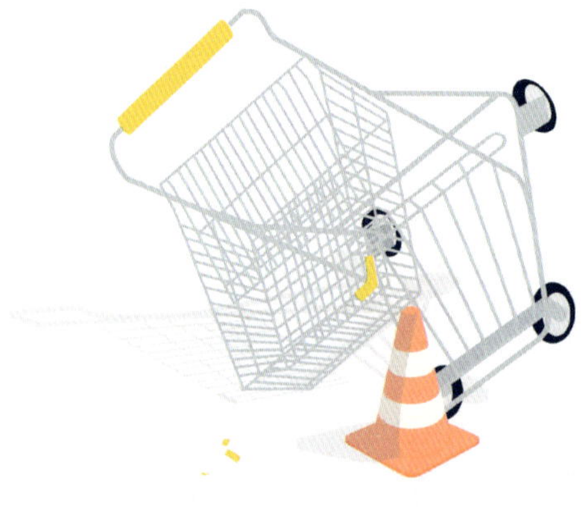

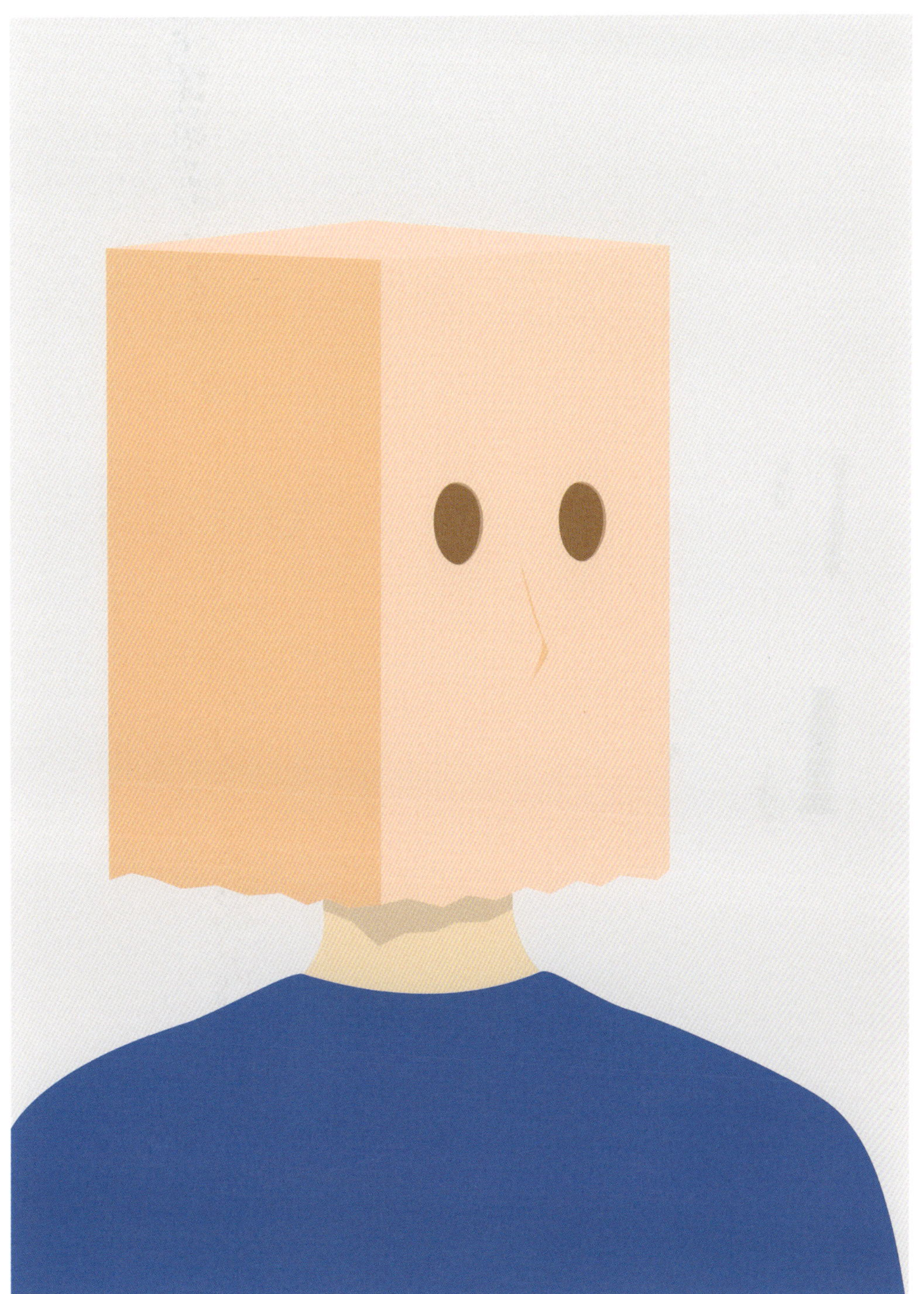

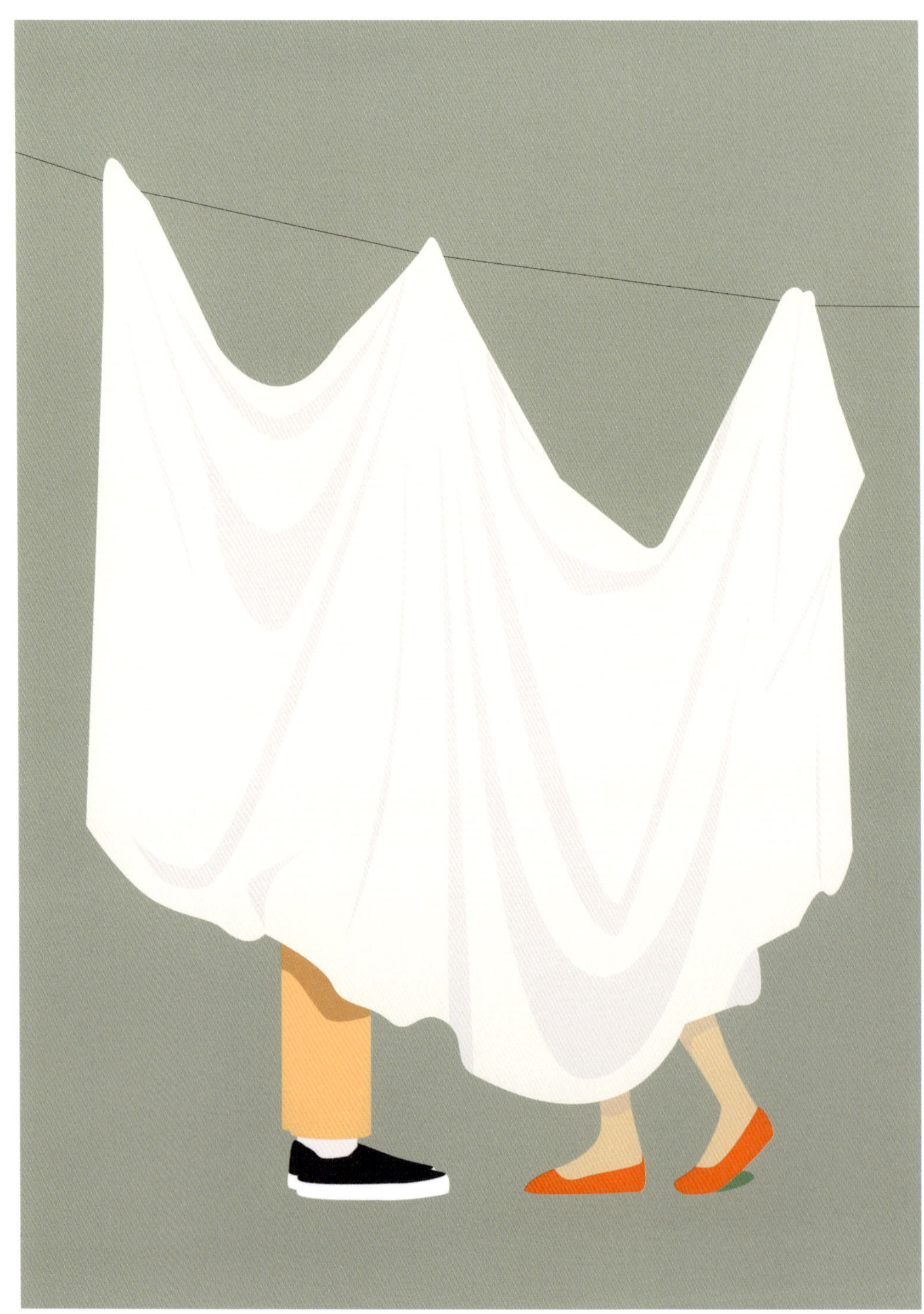

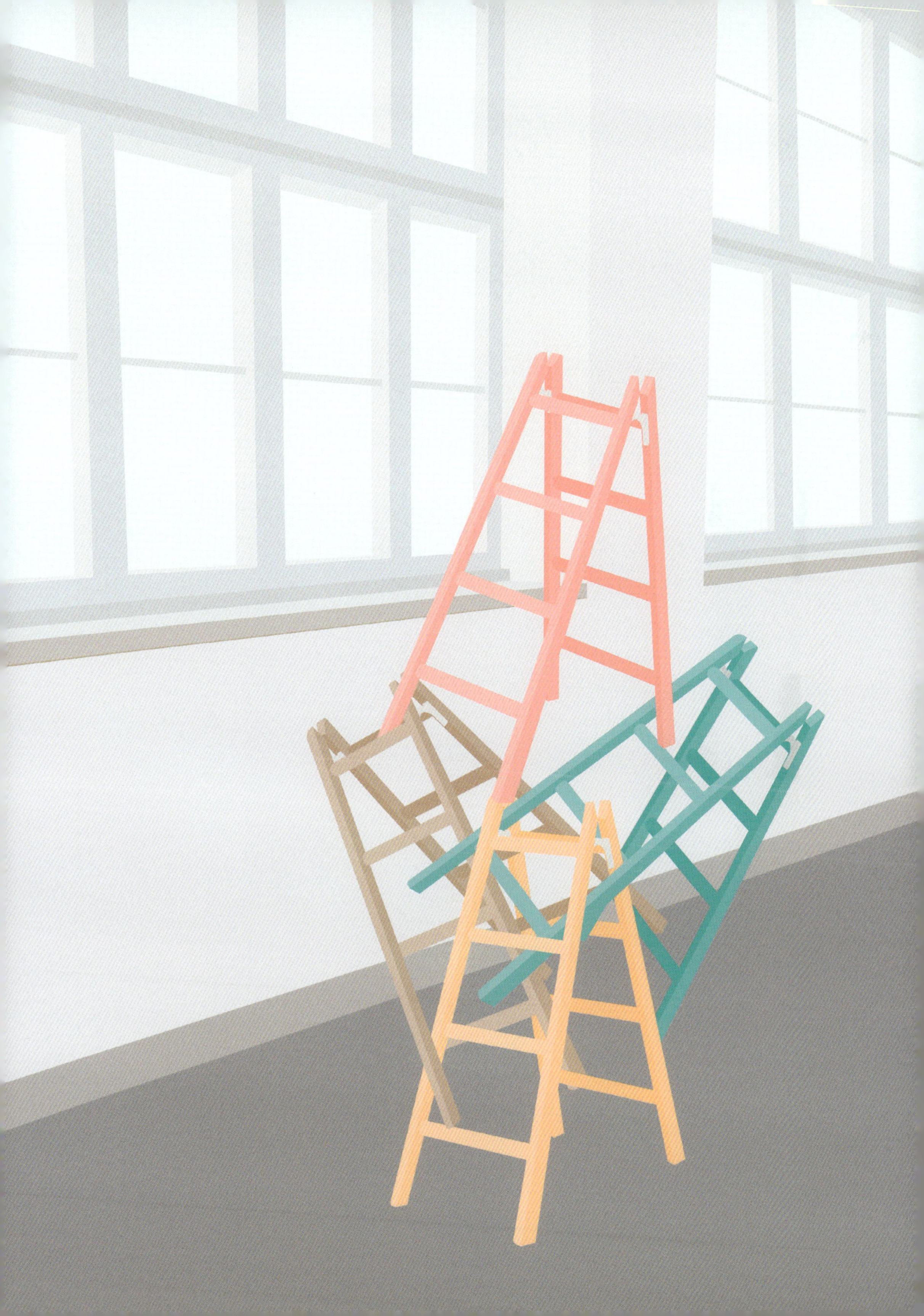

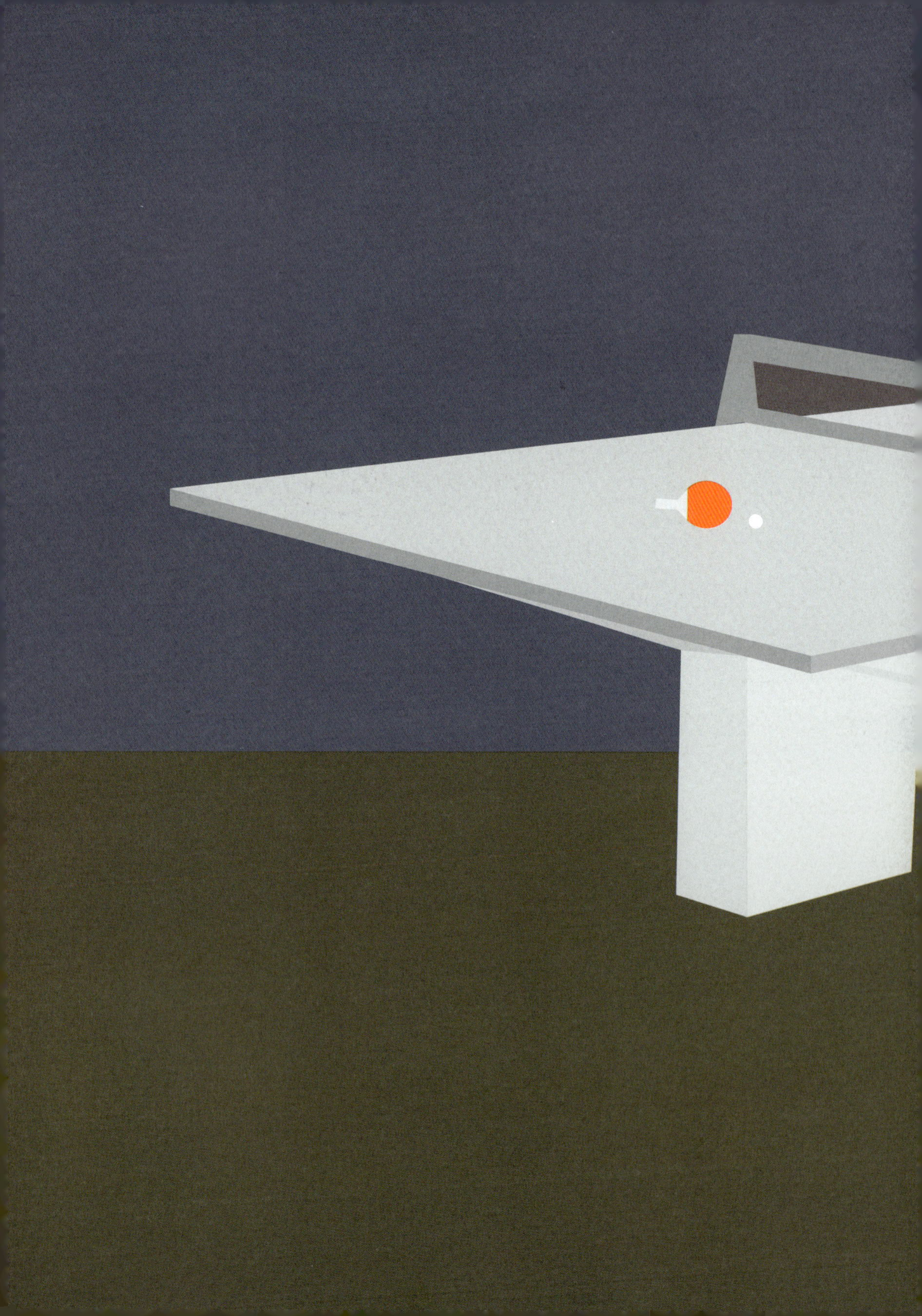

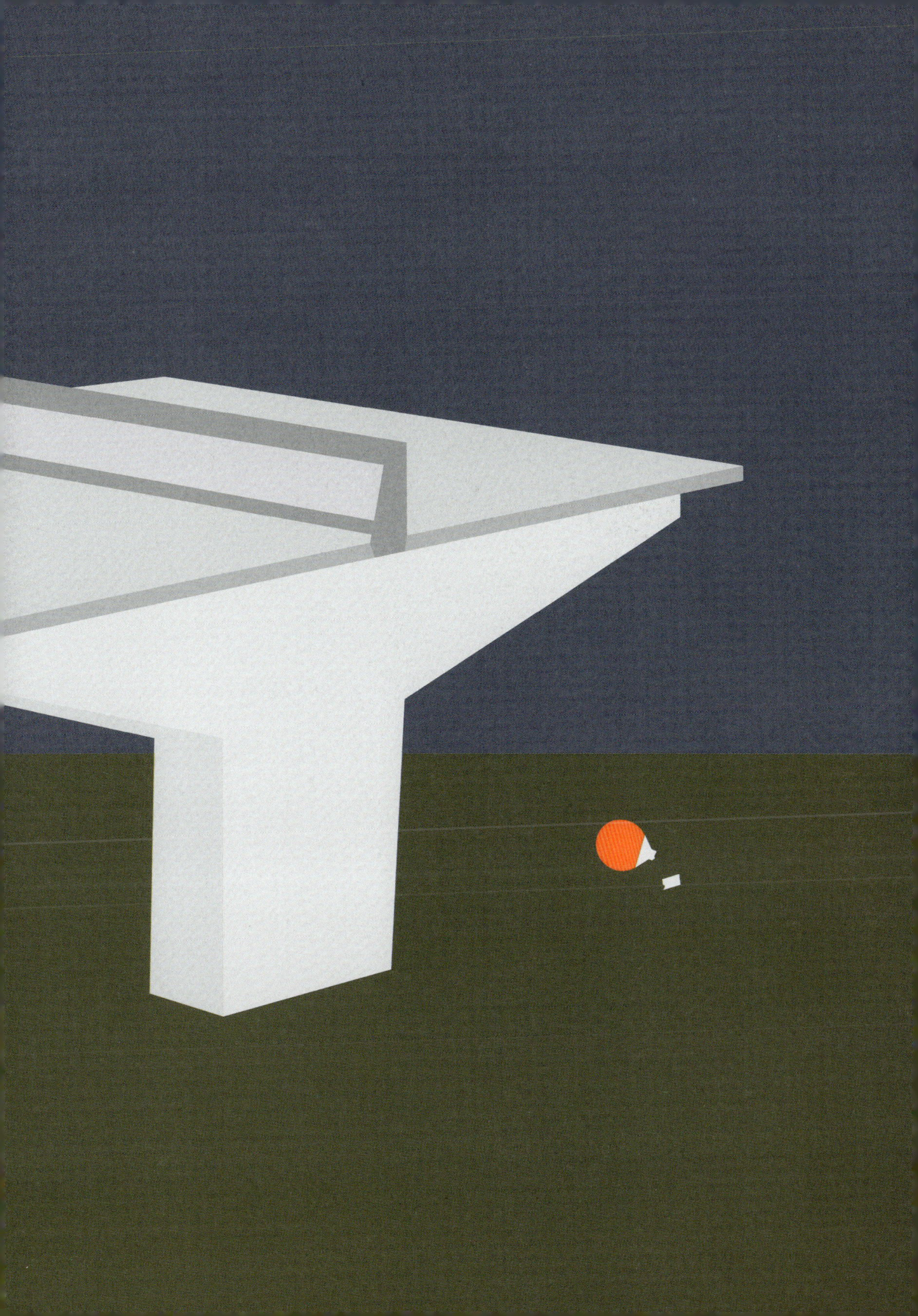

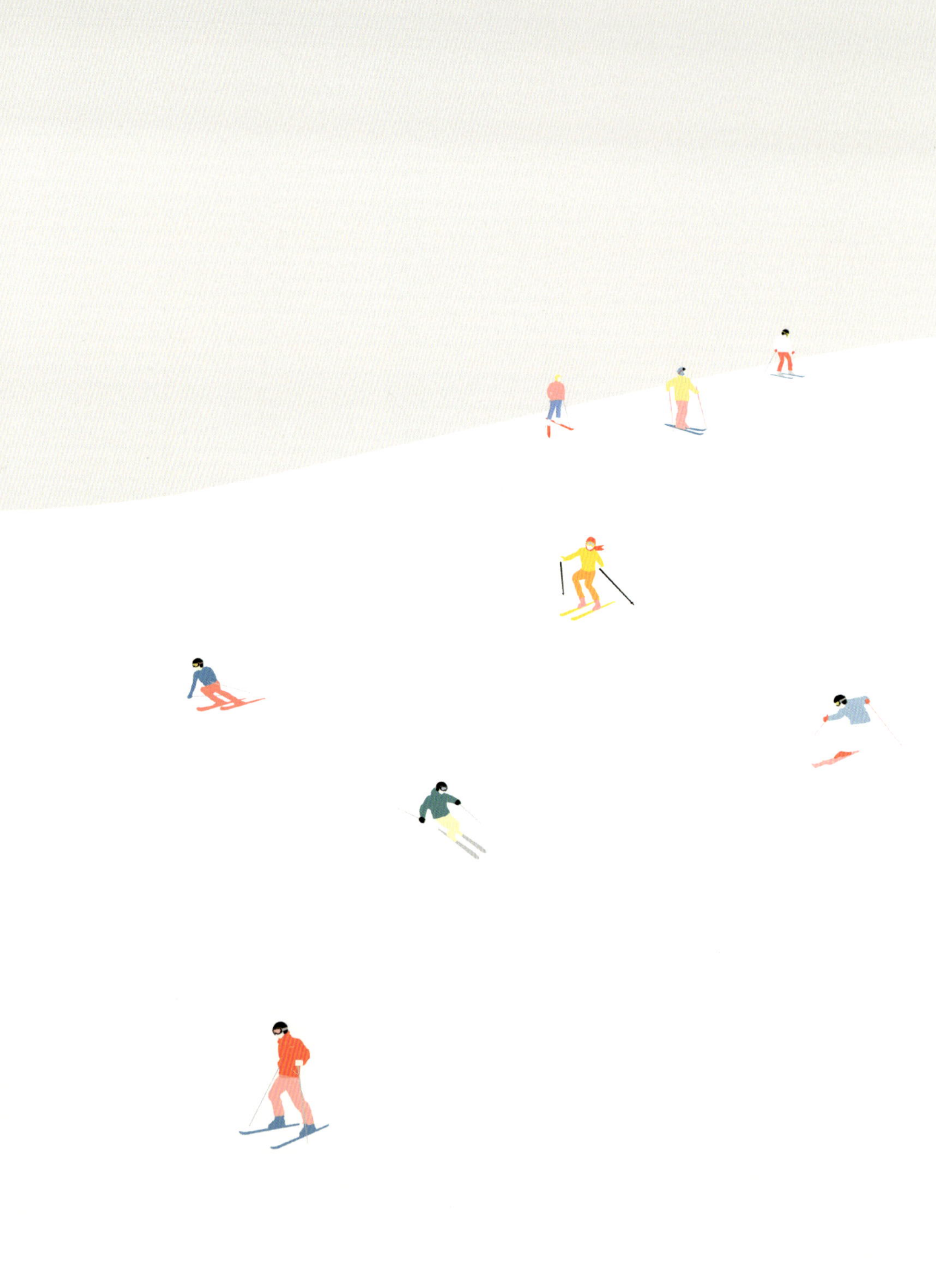

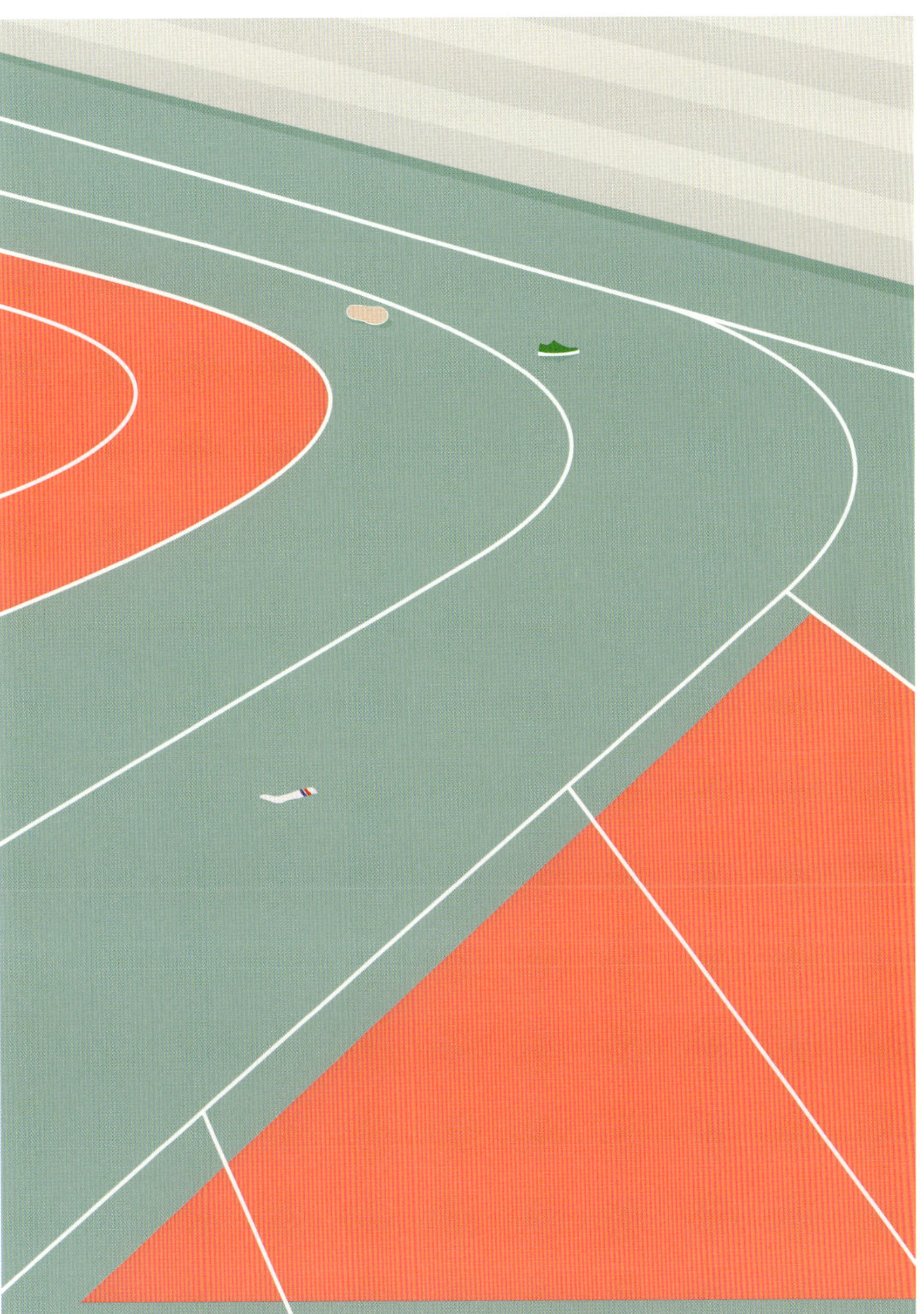

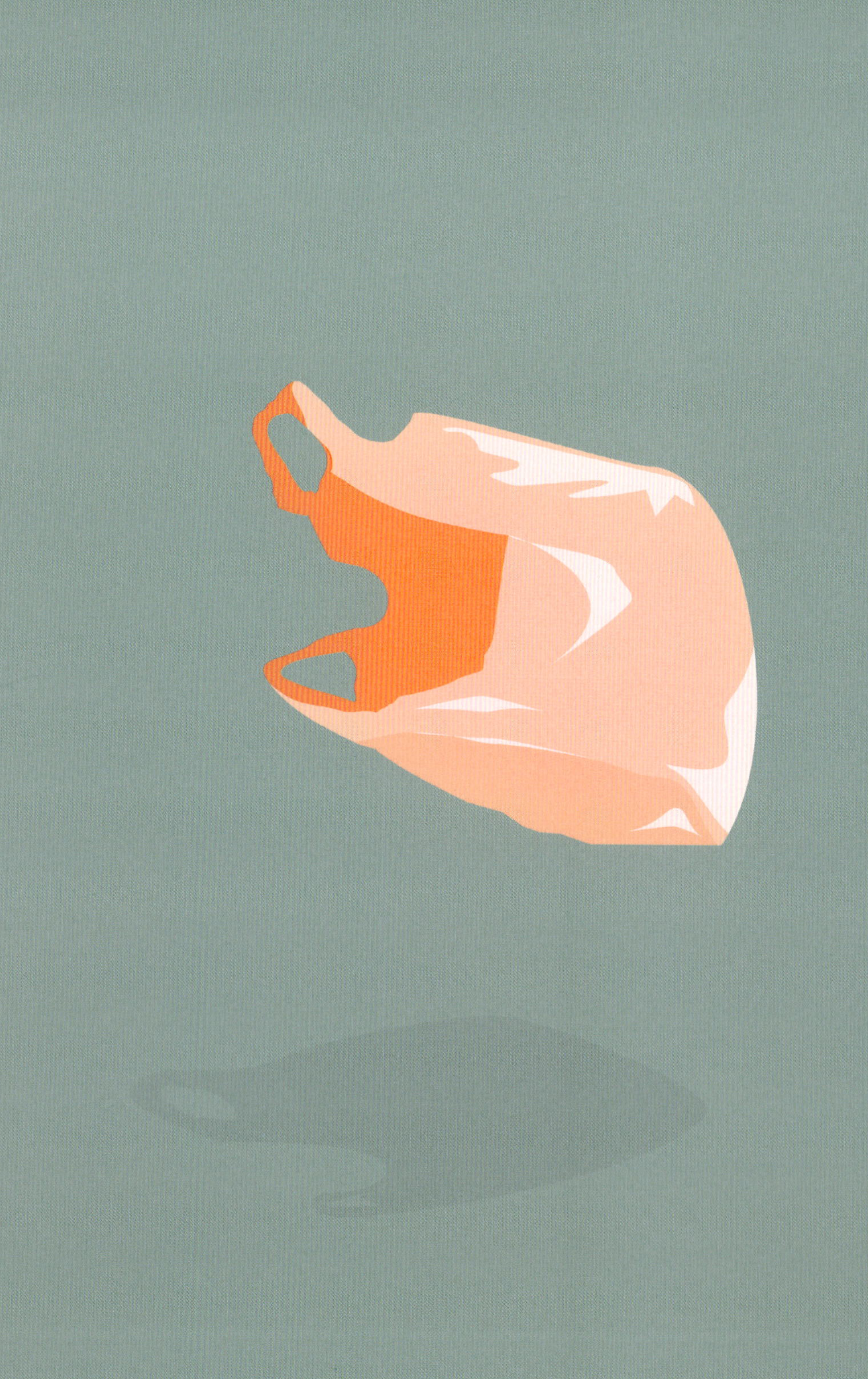

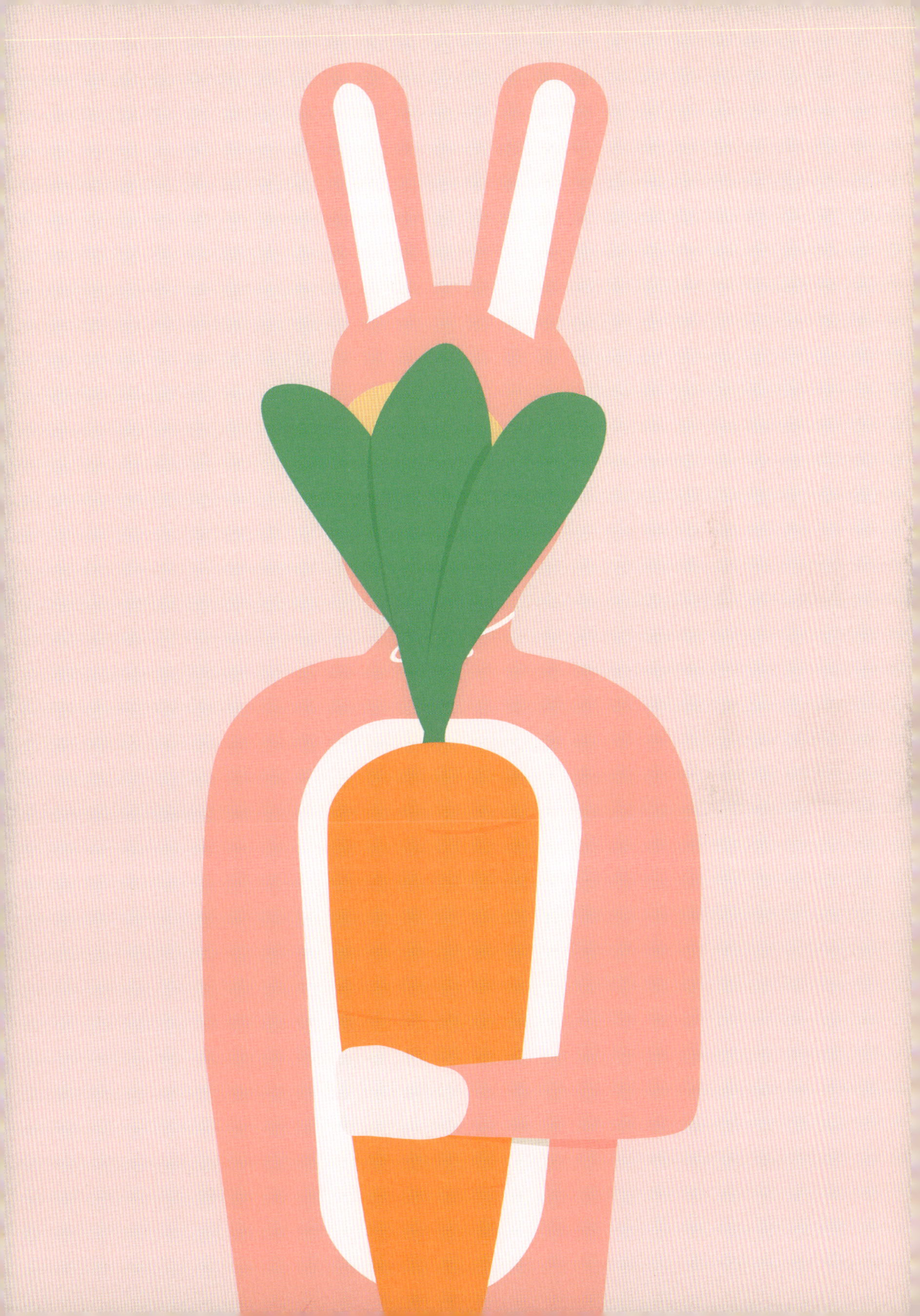

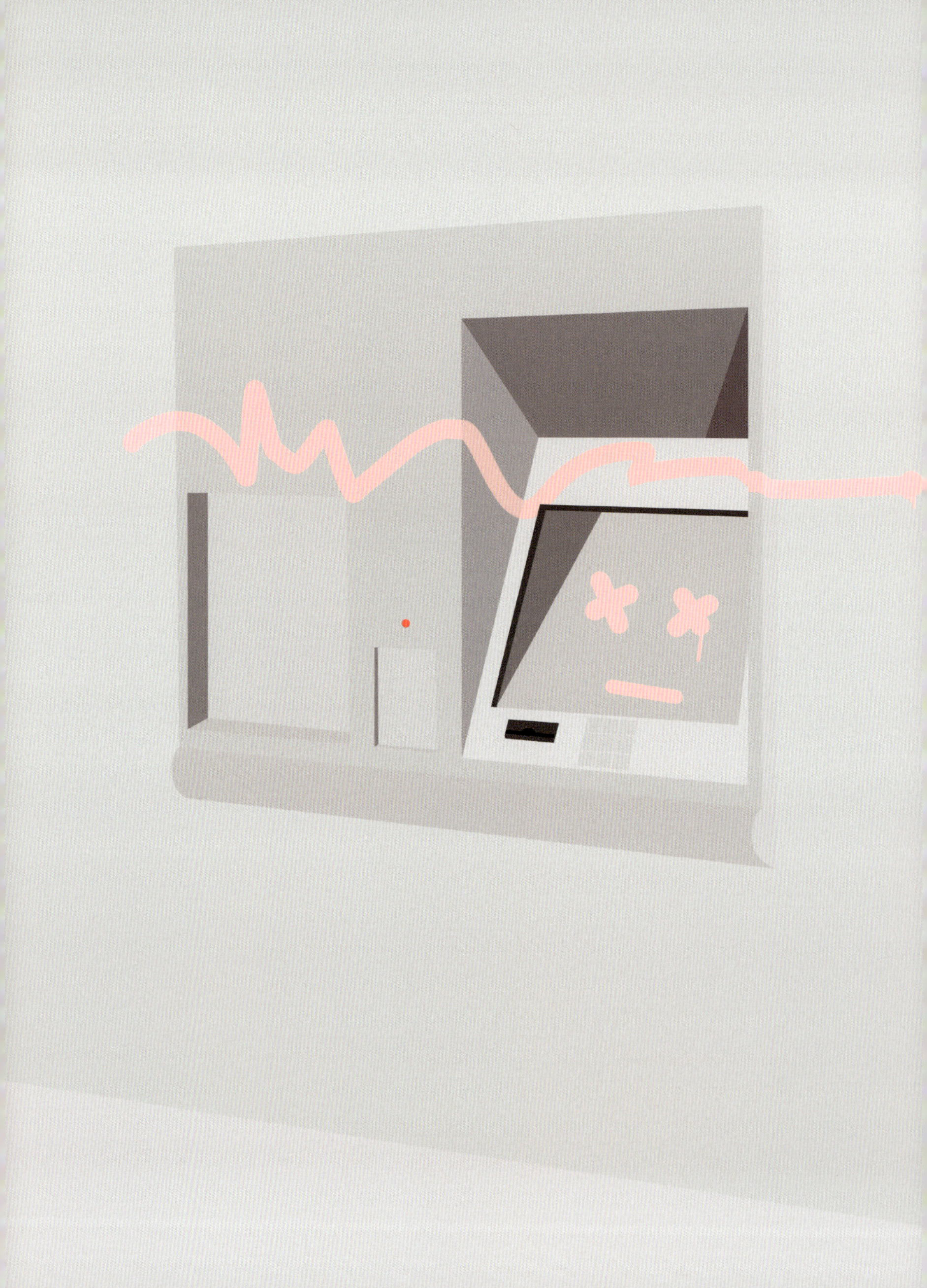

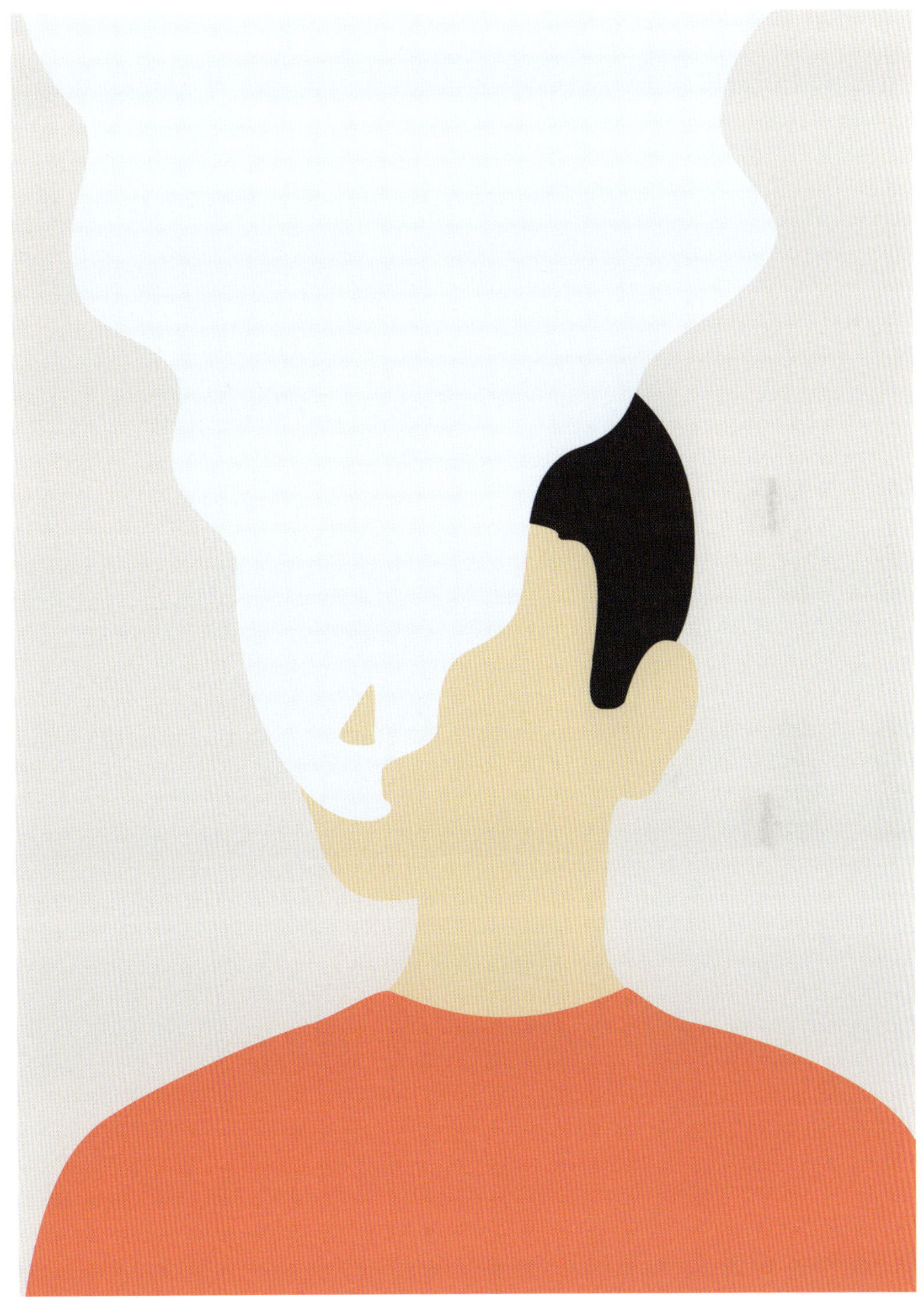

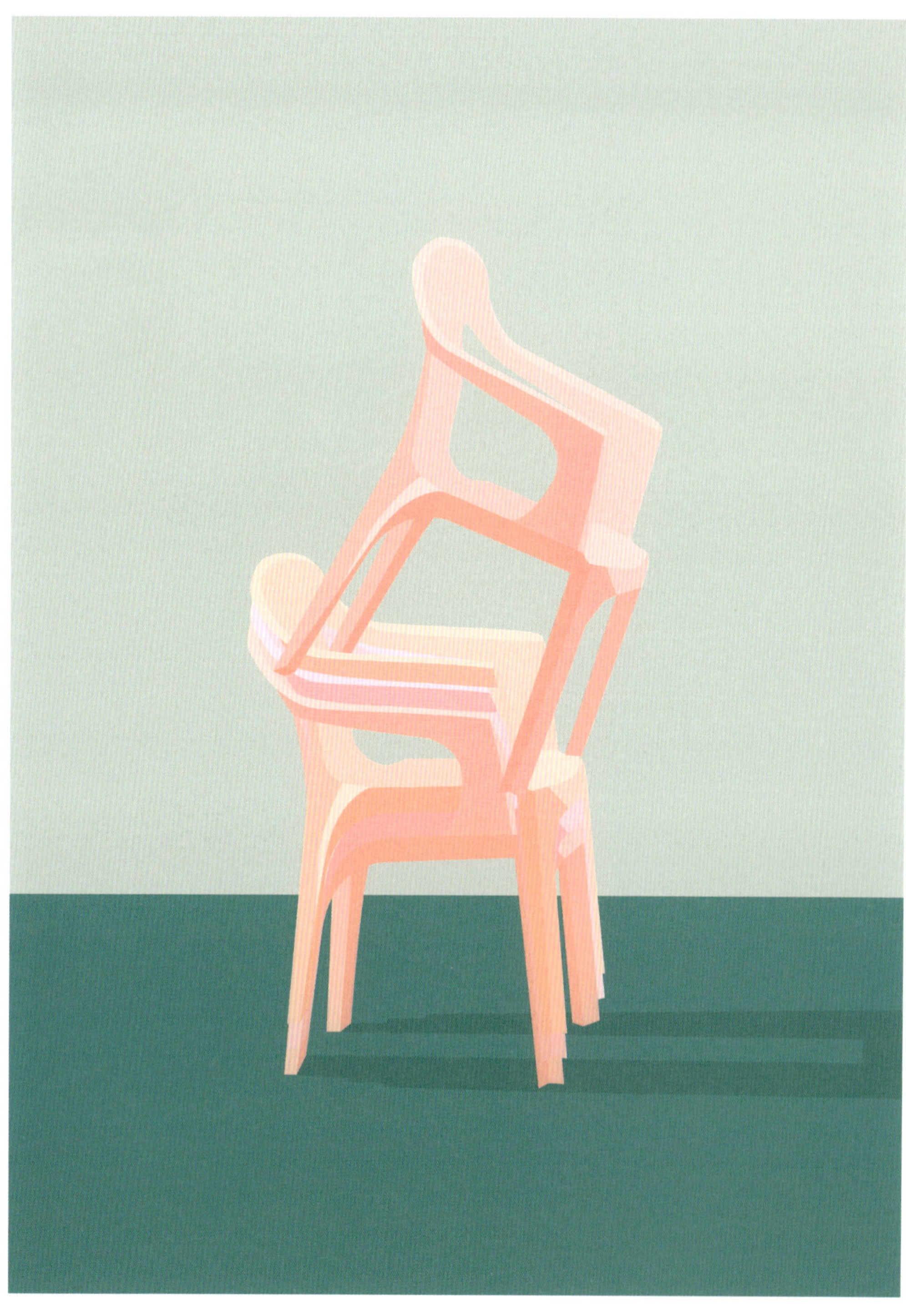

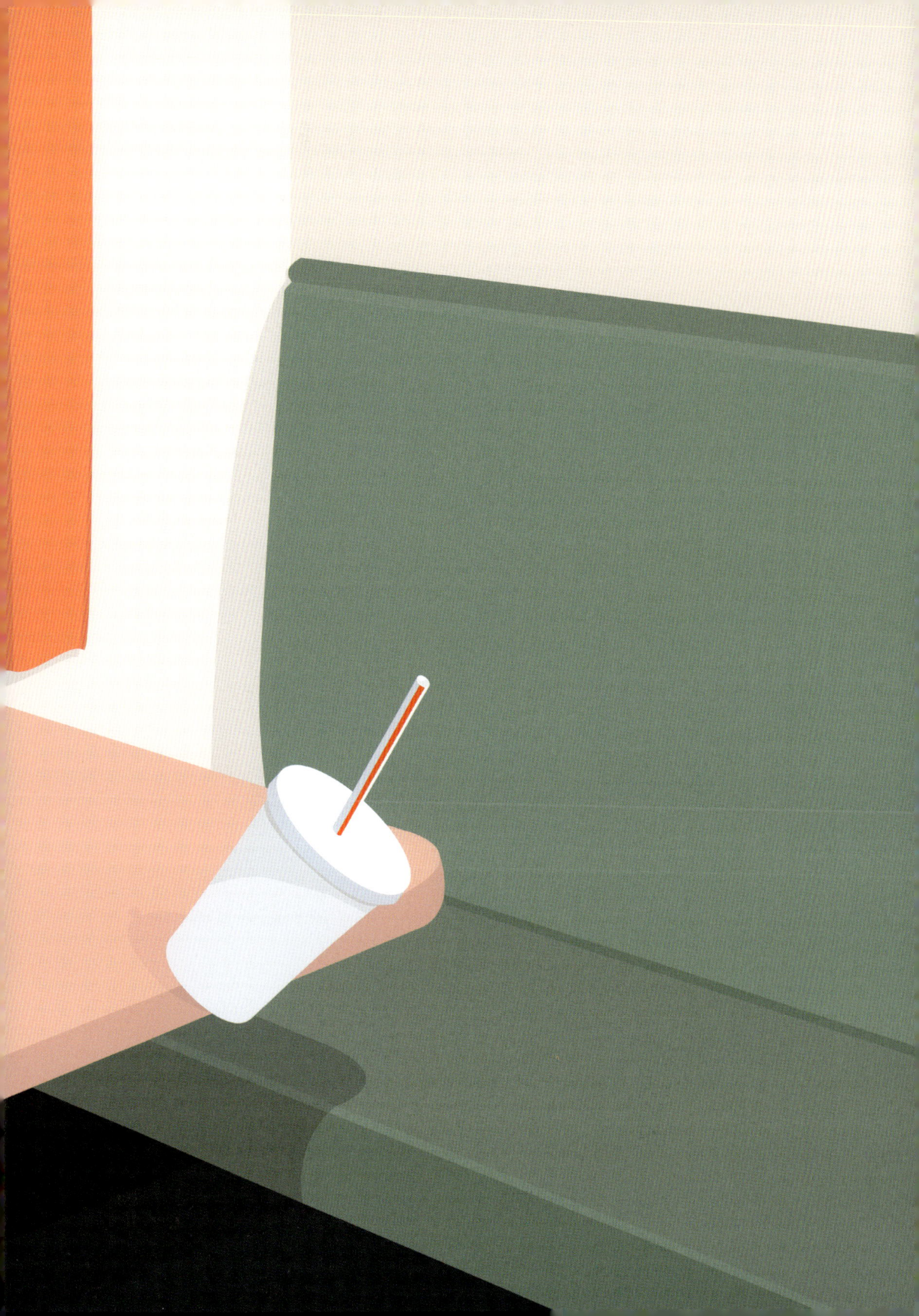

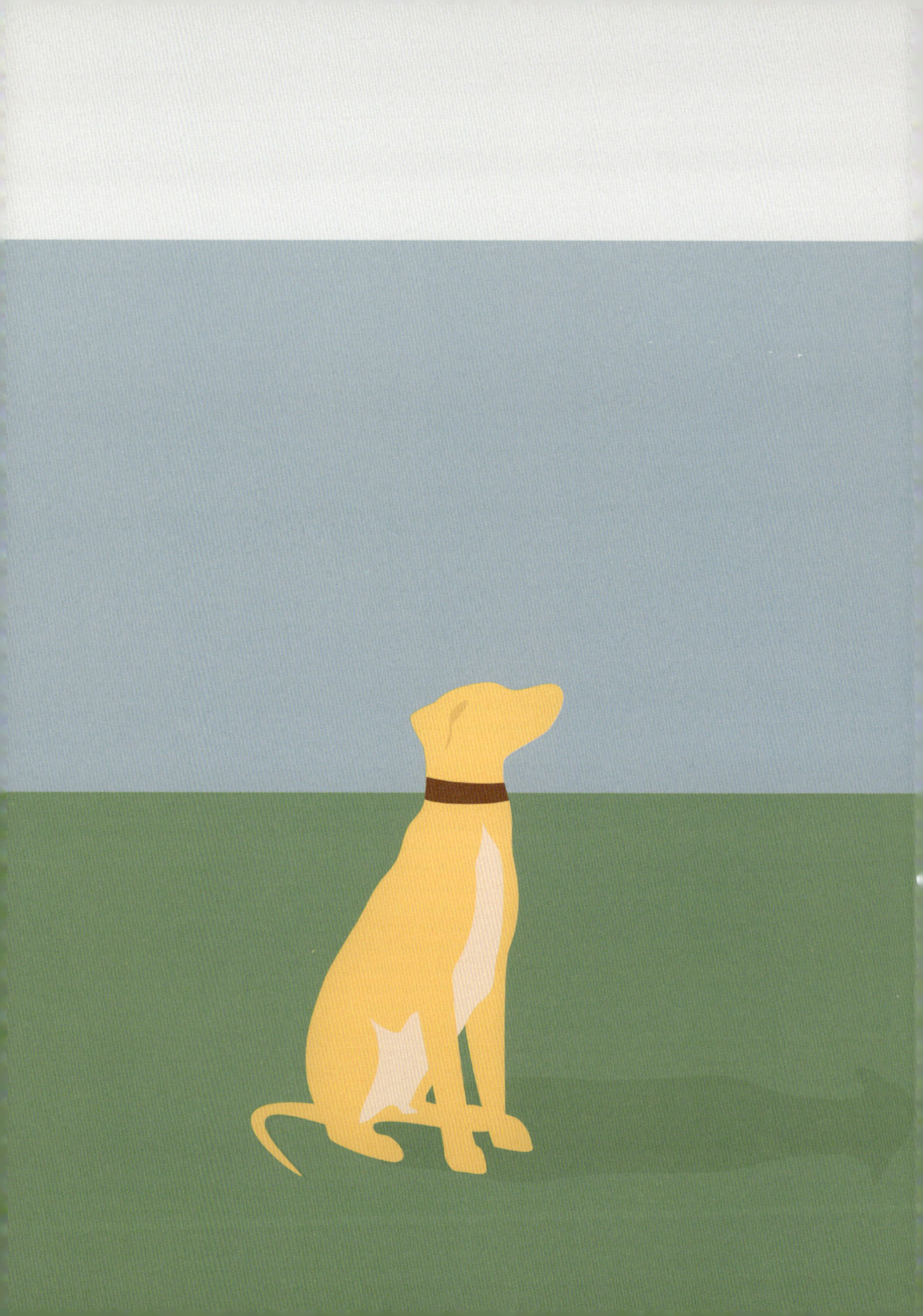

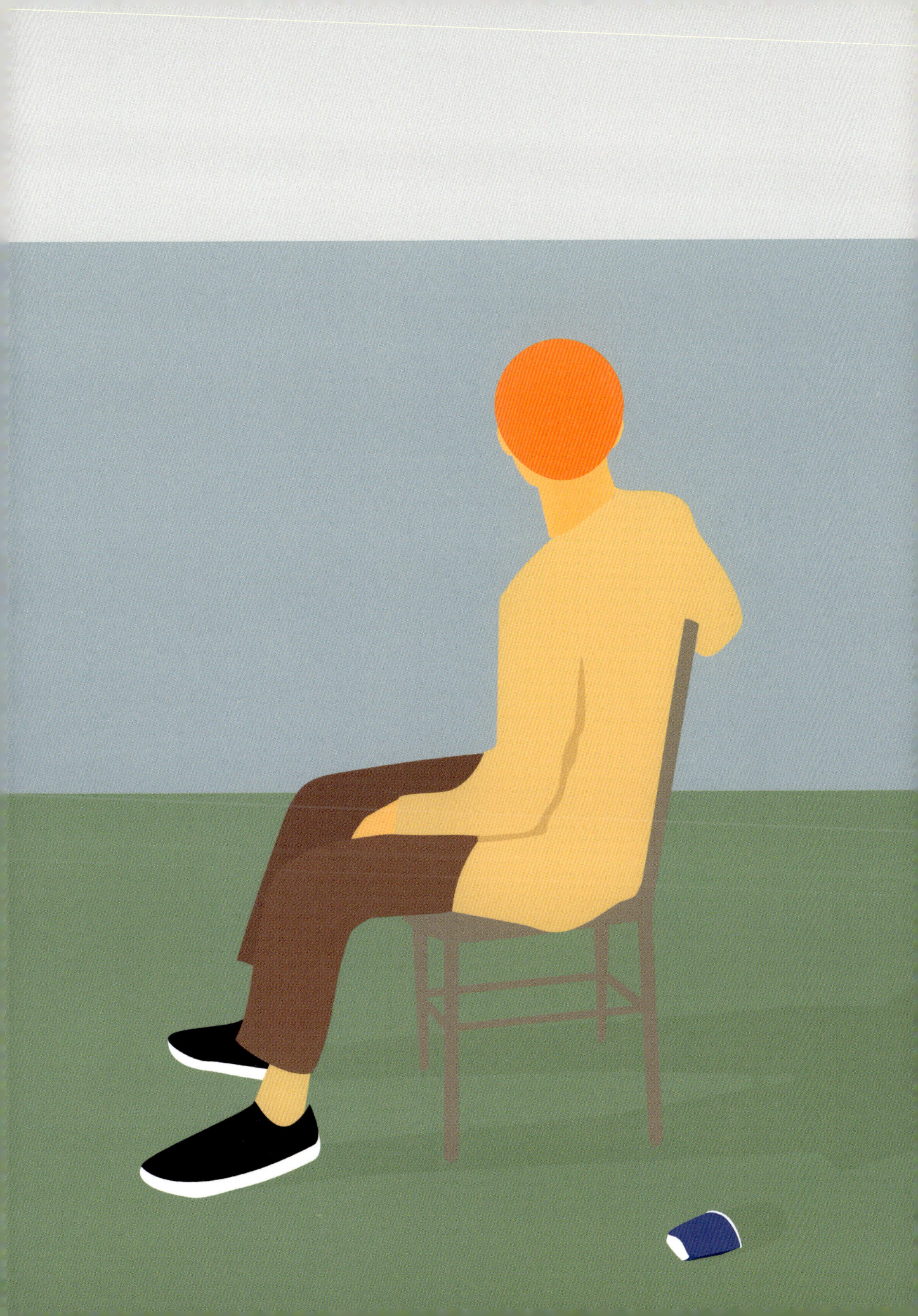

THE ORDINARY AND THE ODD

Published by New Heroes & Pioneers
Illustrations: Swen Swensøn
Creative Direction: Francois Le Bled
Book Design: Daniel Zachrisson
Copy Editing: Matt Porter

Printed and bound by Balto print (Lithuania)
Legal deposit November 2018
ISBN 978-91-87815-36-2

COLLECTIVE SHORTS
by NHP PUBLISHING